UNLIMITED MEMORY POWER

HOW TO REMEMBER MORE, IMPROVE YOUR CONCENTRATION AND DEVELOP A PHOTOGRAPHIC MEMORY IN 2 WEEKS. + BONUS: 21 PRACTICAL MEMORY IMPROVEMENT EXERCISES AND TECHNIQUES

SCOTT SHARP

© Copyright 2020 - All rights reserved.

The content contained within this book may not be reproduced, duplicated or transmitted without direct written permission from the author or the publisher.

Under no circumstances will any blame or legal responsibility be held against the publisher, or author, for any damages, reparation, or monetary loss due to the information contained within this book, either directly or indirectly.

Legal Notice:

This book is copyright protected. It is only for personal use. You cannot amend, distribute, sell, use, quote or paraphrase any part, or the content within this book, without the consent of the author or publisher.

Disclaimer Notice:

Please note the information contained within this document is for educational and entertainment purposes only. All effort has been executed to present accurate, up to date, reliable, complete information. No warranties of any kind are declared or implied. Readers acknowledge that the author is not engaging in the rendering of legal, financial, medical or professional advice. The content within this book has been derived from various sources. Please consult a licensed professional before attempting any techniques outlined in this book.

By reading this document, the reader agrees that under no circumstances is the author responsible for any losses, direct or indirect, that are incurred as a result of the use of information contained within this document, including, but not limited to, errors, omissions, or inaccuracies.

CONTENTS

Introduction   5

PART I: GETTING TO KNOW YOUR BRAIN

Chapter 1: How Memory and Our Brains Work   11
Chapter 2: Better Focus and Concentration   15
Chapter 3: Effective Everyday Learning Strategies   22
Chapter 4: Advanced Learning Strategies   32

PART II: DEVELOPING PHOTOGRAPHIC MEMORY SKILLS — THE BEGINNER'S GUIDE

Chapter 5: Photographic Memory   55
Chapter 6: Remembering Numbers   59
Chapter 7: Remembering Anniversaries and Dates   63
Chapter 8: Remembering Information   66
Chapter 9: Foreign Language Learning — Memorizing Key Words   70
Chapter 10: High-Speed Memory Tips   77
Chapter 11: Memorizing Game Cards   81
Chapter 12: Tricks to Improve Reading Speed   85

PART III: MEMORY FOODS & MEMORY ACTION PLAN

Chapter 13: The Best Foods to Help You Prevent Alzheimer's Disease and Dementia   93
Chapter 14: A Brain-Enhancing and Memory Improvement Menu   97
Chapter 15: Memory Improvement Action Plan for Two Weeks   101

Chapter 16: 21 Memory Improvement
Exercises   137

Conclusion   159
References   163

INTRODUCTION

Do you want to have a better memory? Do you want to boost your brain so you can learn faster, remember more, and be more productive?

Perhaps you want to have a photographic memory and want to be a superhero who can remember all kinds of information, including facts and details, people's names, and events. Or maybe you want to have more focus and concentration to eliminate wasted time, stress, and mistakes at work.

I have everything you need in this book, *Unlimited Memory Power*. As you read, you will learn actionable steps to get the results you want by improving memory and boosting your memory's capacity. I will also teach you how to train your brain to remember more and think and learn faster, using special memory improvement exercises.

This book presents a plan to train your memory with a challenge for your mind, body, and soul. We offer a total package — diet, exercise, stress relief, and memory tricks to help you remember. After going through this routine with multiple methods, you will have a great memory, just like Helen.

Helen was constantly forgetful, and she didn't understand why. She forgot where she put her car keys, ID, phone numbers, and even failed to recall appointments. It caused her a lot of stress. Then she asked me how she could remember things better. I recommended her to try memorizing lists of information like phone numbers or grocery lists. Besides, I advised her to picture each item on the list or even in a series of numbers. Once she visualized the items on her list, she could not forget them. Then Helen applied this method to her daily routine. It changed her life. She had trained her memory to remember things in the short-term. Therefore, she wouldn't have to worry about losing her keys or purse.

In this book, you will learn basic skills and more advanced strategies, including mnemonic devices, the memory palace, the military method, and much more. I will train you to develop a photographic memory that enables you to remember faces and names, numbers, dates, foreign languages, and even game cards. I will also show you how to improve your reading skills. Also, I will talk about the foods that improve your memory.

I will show you some real-life examples, case studies that illustrate how people put into practice the points explained, with excellent results. These scenarios will give you a clear idea of how to apply the methods we have talked about in this book. To protect the privacy of the individuals, we have chosen to introduce alternate names.

You will find how exciting it is to develop your memory and increase your concentration. I invite you to come on this journey to enhance your brainpower. You should work on improving your memory today, so you can be as sharp as ever. Then you can truly be the most successful and fulfilled version of yourself.

Read on to find out more about how you can remember more, stress less, and enjoy a meaningful and productive life starting right now!

PART I: GETTING TO KNOW YOUR BRAIN

CHAPTER 1: HOW MEMORY AND OUR BRAINS WORK

Memories are an essential part of our lives, holding our past, present, and future. Can you imagine living your life with neither the long-term nor the short-term memory that you possess?

Memory is a pretty remarkable feature of what makes us distinctly human, and it's hard to picture life without it. In this chapter, we will describe how the brain works and contributes to memory development.

What Is Memory?

Memory is our brain's process of storing, encoding, and recalling events and experiences from our lives. Some memories occur in episodes, meaning they relate to different experiences that happen in our lives. These are called episodic memories. The other type of memory is called semantic, which refers to rules, facts, and basic fundamental knowledge that we may acquire each day. Semantic memory can be impacted by neurological illnesses, such as Alzheimer's disease, in which the patient loses essential memories.

There are long-term and short-term memories. Our long-term memories are formed by the thoughts and feelings we have had for a long duration. Long-term memories tend to continue for a period of time because they have profoundly affected us. For example, if we experience feelings of stress and fear, we may recall these experiences instinctively without overthinking it. These memories have a long-lasting impact on us, and they linger for a time without fading much. Long-term memories are also stored deep within our brains. In addition to our long-term memories, there are short-term memories, which include experiences of a shorter time. The shortest type of memory is called working memory, which occurs over a few seconds. We experience the effects of working memory while we are multitasking.

For example, your mom tells you an account number, and you type it on your phone. But at the moment between when you hear it and type it, your working memory is processing and holding the information.

How Do Memories Form in the Brain?

Memories are developed in the brain with a system of neurons, which are in constant communication with one another. Memories come together over time and then when we are awake, they are accessed. When we are not sleeping, our brains absorb new information. Then, when we sleep, the memories we have had throughout the day are consolidated and then mold and shape our long-term memories. Once we wake up, we can immediately recall the information since our brain stores our memories. This is why sleep is essential to help your brain process information and store it properly, so you can remember upon demand.

Where Does Your Brain Store the Memories?

Memory consolidation is a complex process. Our brains store memories in different areas. Explicit memories, such as events, facts, and information (semantic) are consolidated in the hippocampus, the neocortex, and the amygdala. On the other hand, implicit memories, such as rote motor skills, are stored in the basal ganglia and cerebellum (memory). Our short-term memories work using our prefrontal cortex.

Episodic memories occur in the hippocampus. These relate to our story and originate from the different events that occur in our lives. An experiment with Henry Molaison in 1953 revealed a lot about the hippocampus. Molaison had surgery on his hippocampus, which was taken out to treat his epilepsy. Even though he had this surgery done, he lived an additional fifty-five years (memory).

However, the surgery deeply impacted Molaison's memory. He had no short-term memories. Instead, he could only use his working memory for a brief few seconds before he forgot all the things he had done. Because he could not consolidate the information in his brain, he became disabled. As a result, most of the long-term memories he retained were from before his surgery.

Other parts of the brain include the neocortex, which helps sensory perception, fine motor skills, and spatial skills. It also helps a person with language development. Memory transfer takes place at night when memories shift from the hippocampus to the cortex.

Strong memories are formed in the amygdala. Such memories include potent emotions, like fear, grief, or traumatic memories. When you have lost a grandmother, been afraid in a fight-or-flight moment, or other stressful situations, these memories have been stored in the amygdala. These memories are particularly unforgettable and thus are consolidated in areas of the brain that locate intense feelings. Within the amygdala, the brain forms memories, specifically in relation to fear. After a few repetitions, the fearful memories remain in the brain for long durations.

Memory related to emotions, reward-based thoughts, movement, and learning occurs in the basal ganglia. This area of the brain is responsible for developing fine motor skills.

Lastly, the cerebellum reinforces fine motor skills, including typing on a laptop, using a fork and knife, playing the piano or violin, and other related skills. Such skills relate to muscle memory, which makes our body's memory process into physical activity.

CHAPTER 2: BETTER FOCUS AND CONCENTRATION

Want to know the secret of better focus and concentration? Do you find yourself constantly distracted and overwhelmed by the things you have to do? Everyone has a lot on their plates. America is indeed one of the most overworked societies in history, with many responsibilities thrust on everyone's shoulders. Workaholism is rampant, and many people come into work early only to return to their homes late. Consequently, unprecedented numbers of people face constant stress and anxiety associated with longer work schedules, more responsibilities at home, and other factors. With a world that can't stop talking, we may find it is hard to get things done. Let's look at some ways we can cope with the overwhelming nature of life in general.

Find Quiet and Organized Places to Work

In a world that is filled with distractions, we may find ourselves tempted to talk to every person around us. In an open office situation, it makes it a lot harder to get tasks done. There is constant anxiety about completing tasks due to a lot of noise around us. Therefore, finding the time and space where we can be undistracted is crucial.

For freelancers or small business owners, working from home is a pleasure to be enjoyed. Having a quiet and organized workspace is one of the key elements of a successful online business. These days, it is easier than ever to do that from home. When you can carve out for yourself a quiet space that you can enjoy, you can experience more productivity and joy than ever before.

For those of you who work in an office, it often takes perseverance and energy to get through the day. Finding the time to focus requires you to stop talking to others and get down to business. Sometimes, that means saying "no" to informal meetings with people or talking to someone next to you. Staying in your "zone" at work is a vital part of accomplishing all the tasks you need to do.

Practice Mindfulness and Stay in the Present Moment

One helpful practice inspired by Eastern philosophy and meditation is mindfulness. It is becoming more popular in Western societies because it helps you to relax and get things done effectively. When you practice mindfulness, you think about your breathing and posture and other things in your life. You take time out of your schedule and pause for a moment of silence. Within that moment, you close your eyes, get into a comfortable position in your chair, count from one to twenty (or more), and pray, meditate, or think to yourself. Doing so gives you the freedom to think about whatever is on your heart and mind. Then, you can clearly articulate to yourself what you are experiencing in that given moment. It gives you the ability to know yourself and what drives you. Additionally, it enables you to think about the present moment.

Stay Grounded in the Present

Different kinds of people think about reality in contrasting ways. For example, some people are always in the past and regretting the actions of yesterday, last week, a month ago, or a year ago. This type of person is quite miserable and depressed all the time. Likely, they dwell on their mistakes and are hard on themselves. The other type of person overthinks about the future and worries a lot. They may be thinking of what they need to do tomorrow, next week, or next year. Their thoughts are preoccupied with the future so much that they are not mindful of the present. As a result, they are unhappy, preoccupied, and busy.

There is another kind of person, the one who is grounded in the present. That person is happy, content, and at peace. A person who is in the present moment knows the past and does not dwell on it. They also know that there is a future, and they are preparing for it. However, they don't worry about what is going to happen. Instead, they make sure to enjoy what they are doing at the moment. They don't allow precious time to be wasted because they know their time on earth is limited. Therefore, they try to do things that are beneficial to them. They appreciate what they have and are thankful. They are not motivated by power or money. Instead, they value simplicity. Living a simple life, they are full of joy and fulfillment in their present circumstances, regardless of whatever they are. They find meaning in their work and relationships with people and are a lot of fun to be around.

Better Concentration Techniques

Recognizing that distracting environments can be unavoidable, we also need to find ways to manage those environments, maximizing our effectiveness despite the distraction. Want to know some concentration techniques that can strengthen your mental capacities? Let's look at some of them (McKay and McKay, 2019).

1. Meditate

You don't have to be a Buddhist monk or go to a monastery to meditate and enjoy the benefits of it. Meditating can have a powerful impact on our minds throughout the day since we feel more relaxed. We are able to absorb information and reflect on how we are thinking and feeling. When you meditate, you will also find that you can regulate your emotions more efficiently, and it makes you feel on top of your game. Meditation is one thing that should be integrated throughout your day for the best results.

2. Memorize Things. Practice!

Memorization is an exercise that you should practice regularly. To keep your mind in top shape, you should practice memorizing anything in your life. It may be numbers in the phone book or places on a map — anything that floats your boat. Try to find something that you really enjoy memorizing. It will help you enhance your concentration powers.

3. Exercise

Exercise can be a powerful tool to help students succeed on exams. It has proven health benefits, not only physically but mentally, as well. Moderate intensity exercise releases feel-good chemicals called endorphins in our brains, which helps regulate emotions and boosts our self-esteem. Additionally, when we exercise our bodies, we also improve our memory and help ourselves remember things better. Exercise can also have meditative qualities. For example, swimming laps in a pool can be a meditative activity in which you can engage your whole body.

4. Read Slowly

Another thing we need to do is read words slowly. In an age where information can be consumed instantly without thinking or reflecting, we have a lot of data at our fingertips. However, when we read information on a screen, tablet, or phone, we might lose sight of things. Sometimes, the blue light from the screen can cause us to have reduced sleep ability at night. But when you read low-tech in a paperback book, you will find that as you slow down to learn something, you can retain more. Plus, you allow yourself to process the information more quickly and efficiently. Slow yourself down.

5. Stay Curious About the World. Research!

Another point you must always do is remain curious about the world. Never stop learning. Always be growing. Read the news. Do internet searches on different topics. Become an expert on a topic of your choice. When you read widely and study things, then you can develop your mindset and discover many new things. Research various subjects online and in print. You will find that many options are waiting to be read in the world. Reading is an important skill that you can take with you for the rest of your life.

6. Practice Attentive Listening

In this distracted world, we need to have more people with active listening skills. Often, even as you speak in a conversation, the other person may be about to take a phone call or text someone else. It is rude and not caring toward the other person when you do this. It is important to be present in a given moment. When someone is talking to you, give them your full attention. It shows you are respectful toward them and that you want to hear what they have to say. When anyone is talking to you, don't get distracted and multitask to do other things. Instead, truly listen to what the other person has to say to you. It will change your life. You must try to do this as much as possible, because then you can be present for another person and build trust with them. It greatly enhances your life.

CHAPTER 3: EFFECTIVE EVERYDAY LEARNING STRATEGIES

Here are some basic strategies that will help you remember almost anything you need to recall.

Use Your House and Car to Remember

One good idea for remembering things is to use the different spaces you live in and use regularly. When you can remember where you put things, you can always make sure to be mindful of what you're doing when you place an item somewhere.

For example, say you're putting your glasses on the coffee table. You can remember you put your glasses in that location by saying to yourself, "I was brushing my teeth when I put my glasses on the coffee table."

Just saying those words aloud will help you verbalize your thoughts of the glasses and make the association with the coffee table. You will then likely not lose your glasses again. Instead, you will have made the audiovisual word association and incorporated the spatial aspect, which helps you to see, hear, and speak the word.

Another option you can do is try to visualize different things as having a place in your home. You can label them in different parts of your home or room and then you can bring those to life in your memory. You can easily recall where everything is and deconstruct the rooms of your home, so you can find whatever it is you have placed there. It will help you stay organized and keep everything in good order in your home.

You can do the same thing with your car. You can use your car to help you remember where different things are. For example, you can visualize items in your glove compartment, in the back seat, or in the trunk. You can use your audiovisual and spatial-temporal memory to help you locate all the things in your car, which will help you remember well.

Use Your Body to Remember

In addition to your car and home, you can also use your body to remember things. For example, if you have a friend named Melanie, and you want to remember her name and face, you can make an association. You could think "melon" and "knee," and you could physically point to your knee at the time of speaking. Making this connection right away will enable you to remember things faster and more efficiently.

Try to find the best way to make such associations. It will help you a lot.

When you have to memorize a list of items you need to buy at the grocery store, you can also use this technique to remember everything. For example, if you have to buy several items, such as milk, eggs, cheese, cat food, and bread, you could use your body to be the placemaker for each part of this list. You could say something like "I'm lifting milk and eggs with my hands and cheese on my knees with cat food on my back and bread on my thigh." You could even make up some story. In the end, you will succeed in remembering all the key information.

In addition to this information you need to memorize, you can also use your body to remember things. One necessary way is to write notes on your hand to help you remember better. Sometimes, putting a symbol on the hand can also make remembering a lot easier.

Linking Your Thoughts to Make Associations

One of the great ways of remembering information is making word associations, which help you to memorize all things. For example, you might have a list of words on a piece of paper. They have absolutely nothing in common, but you must create some semblance of order and organization to bring them together for better retention. What can you do? Try to make a visual story with everything on the list. Let's look at a basic example of how this works with a list of random words.

Turkey
Family
Order
Tree
Talking
Fruit
TV
Complaint
Warm
Raining

To bring together this list of items, you make an association. Here's an example story: There is a **turkey** in the oven. It is Thanksgiving and a **family** of four is sitting at the table. The lady of the house is taking everyone's **order.** There is a **tree** outside that the family is planning on cutting down for a Christmas tree. Everyone is **talking** and having a good time. The **TV** is on and showing the Braves game. But the husband makes a **complaint** after complaint about the umpires and their calls. Overall, it is **warm** inside, though it is **raining** outside.

Word associations have long been a useful way of remembering things. It is not enough to remember things using rote memorization. You have to find a way to connect ideas. No two things can be disconnected from each other. One of the reasons why many memorization tactics fail is because things are not placed in a context. When you can put words together contextually, then it becomes easier to remember all the items on a list. In many countries, students must rely on their rote memorization skills, which can help them ace a test. But it is not a reliable method to help them remember something for life. But if a person connects ideas in a sentence, story, or paragraph, then they can remember words and other items well.

Another word association game you can try is creating a jingle for the words that you want to put together. That involves making a song with music. You can do the song with your favorite tune and sing it out loud. After you have learned this song, you will immediately make the associations in the content and be able to remember everything. Hannah Montana (Miley Cyrus) did this in her series, as she did the Bone Dance to remember anatomical terms of the bones of the human body. By incorporating a total body experience, she, along with her other classmates, successfully recalled the information in the song to ace a test.

It is crucial to come up with creative and innovative ways to memorize items. If we don't make it a little bit fun, it can be dry and boring to learn something. We need to motivate ourselves to do something. Grades motivate many students on a test. What's more, it is important to be excited about the right reasons and that includes lifelong learning. This should be the goal for education: to help students realize their potential and succeed in this globalized world.

Pegging Memory Information System

Another method we can incorporate in our routine is pegging information. For example, when you use numbers, you can associate the figure with a word that has the same vowel sound as that number. Then, you can easily create images that bring everything together so you can remember better. Let's look at an example of how you can do that with numbers from 0 to 9 (Pegging Memory System, n.d.).

1-fun
2-true
3-see
4-store
5-alive
6-sticks
7-heaven
8-fate
9-fine
0-foe

You can use these numbers to form images, which will help you remember the data better. For example, if it is a phone number or zip code, you can recall instantly after having formed sentences with it. Let's look at a concrete example. Say, we want to remember the following number: 567821. Then, we can make the following association.

The man was **alive (5)**. He ate some cheese **sticks (6)** and thought they tasted like **heaven (7)**. It was **fate (8)** that he would meet his **true (2)** love and have a **fun (1)** time.

As you can see, by assembling this information into a story, you can bring everything together and remember the number.

Improving Memory While Sleeping

One of the essential things in our lives is sleep. Getting enough rest each night is crucial to helping us feel at our best. If we don't get enough sleep at night, we will not feel right and rely on caffeine or other stimulants to get us going. Additionally, much of our long-term memory is consolidated in our brains at night when we doze off. Therefore, sleep is a necessity for us to store memories in our minds.

Aside from getting enough rest to restore our bodies, we need brainpower from our sleep to get us through the day. Otherwise, it will be impossible for us to remember the items on our list. If you want to remember more, you should catch more z's. It will help you experience more freedom and flexibility than ever before.

There is a saying that we remember more when we "sleep on" something. In fact, an adage mentions that we can learn a skill or piece of information in our sleep. This saying has some truth to it. When we get enough sleep, our memory retains more information, which makes it easier for us to recall things on a test, in a competition, or in a speech.

If we don't get enough sleep, our memory will be spotty, and we might forget a lot of things. In addition, we will not feel up to par. Getting enough sleep at night also affects our moods and how we feel. It is vital to receive enough rest at night, because then we can be at our best and perform well on whatever task we are given.

Furthermore, the more we sleep, the more our brain can store the information we take in every day of our lives. We are indeed inundated with sensory data in all forms in our daily routine. Therefore, we need to make time to sleep and allow our brains to consolidate all the vital information that we need to survive and thrive.

How to Deal with Forgetting

With all the busyness of our lives, we are prone to forget basic things. Unfortunately, it is a part of being human. However, there are ways we can train and discipline ourselves to avoid forgetting about things. Let's look at some basic ways to deal with forgetfulness, which will help you to recall all the essential information in your life (Chernyak, 2019).

1. Organize your time and schedule.

One of the basic ways you can avoid forgetting things is by organizing your schedule. Have a set time for all aspects in your life, including wake-up and bedtime, among other things. You should also write notes down all the time because then you will not forget easily.

2. Create a to-do list and stick to it.

Secondly, you should create a to-do list and stick to it. Whether that is a physical hardcopy or a virtual mobile list, you can write down all the things you need to accomplish in one day. As you go, you can check off each completed task. It helps you stay organized and makes it easier for you to remember.

3. Set alerts on your phone and computer.

If you are afraid of missing a deadline or appointment, put an alert on your phone or computer that lets you know when an important event is about to happen Then, you will be sure not to forget this important information. You will immediately remember and do what you need to do.

4. Avoid procrastination.

Next, you should avoid waiting until the last minute to do anything. Procrastination is a common problem, and it is something you should try to minimize in your life. Procrastinators experience a lot of stress and anxiety. Some people operate well under pressure, but most people freak out and have a panic attack. Therefore, it is crucial for your mind's sake to stop procrastinating, get yourself organized, and do all the tasks that require your attention. Set personal deadlines for yourself and daily goals that are achievable. This will help you avoid procrastination.

5. Stay focused.

Finally, identify any distractions that might be causing you to forget things. Often, we are distracted by the bells and whistles of this world, including notifications on our phones. These distractions do not help us as we're memorizing vital information. Furthermore, we need to have ways of focusing our attention. If that means turning off our phones, computers, or other devices, then that's what we should do. Disconnecting from technology is ideal but is not always possible. But it can be an efficient way of getting us to focus on one task at a time. Most people are not meant to be multitaskers. It is best to be present in the given moment so as to not forget what we are doing and accomplish more. Often, it takes doing less so we can achieve more.

CHAPTER 4: ADVANCED LEARNING STRATEGIES

In this chapter, you will learn about how to remember almost anything under the sun using various strategies that will enhance your active memory. Let's look at several of those methods.

Using All Five Senses

When you're learning something for the first time, it is helpful to use all your senses whenever possible. When you learn new information, take note of the sensory information that surrounds the material you learn — all the colors, sounds, smells. These will help you to inscribe it in your memory. You may be a visual learner, able to remember things when you see them in front of your eyes. But practice engaging all of your senses. For example, to activate your memory, you might say aloud the things you want to remember whenever you view them on a piece of paper.. You could even put some rhythm or music to it, which will enable you to remember even better. Sing or recite the items on your to-do list like a poem. It will help you remember and allow you to increase your powers of concentration.

Example

Jeric was active in engaging his senses as he was studying for a chemistry exam in college. He had to remember all the chemical formulas for the exam. It was very tough for him. However, he was able to remember when he did the twin tasks of writing everything down and then reciting it out loud. He even created a chant and song that he could recall at any given time. He would remember these formulas for a long time afterward.

Connect Things with Background Knowledge

Often we learn things better when we can apply our background knowledge. Whether that is having the same birthdate as another person or wearing the same color of clothing, we form associations in mind based on our background knowledge. When you are learning new information, try to connect it to something that you have already learned before. It will significantly aid your memory and help you learn things a lot faster.

Example

Say you are learning to drive a car. You go to driving school, read the manuals, and attend the lectures. Now you have all that background knowledge. You will learn how to do that by actually being in a car and driving. It helps you to apply all that you learn. To be sure, you will need a fair amount of practice to put together all of that background knowledge effectively as a safe driver. But when you do, you will intuitively remember nearly all of the rules and procedures you learned in the abstract.

Mnemonic Devices

Our memories are intended to be shaped by how we associate words with them. Through associating images with words, we can construct meaning and make memories. One way to do this is through using mnemonic devices, which help us to remember almost anything.

Many times, we cannot remember basic things because we haven't trained our minds to recall the proper way. Furthermore, we frequently forget how to do things because we rely on our rote memory to remember the basic facts and figures of our lives. However, this method is ineffective and doesn't work the way it should. What we should think about is how we can apply memory concepts to our everyday lives.

Mnemonic devices have been used since ancient times to help people remember things. The word "mnemonic" comes from the Greek term, *mnemonikos*, which means "to be mindful," ("Mnemonic," n.d.). Mnemonic devices help people to remember clearly. When you use these tools, you will be able to encode something so it is stored in your memory permanently. As a result, you will be able to recall things on demand in no time. Let's look at some examples of mnemonic devices.

The Method of Loci

The method of loci allows you to imagine yourself in a familiar place, like your house or neighborhood. You use these common places to store your memories. For instance, you read through a list of terms that you are required to memorize and then you put each of these words in the different areas of the familiar place. This method enables you to memorize many things. Then, you will be able to review this information whenever you want ("Memory and Mnemonic Devices," n.d.). I will provide some specific applications of this method later in this chapter.

Acronyms

For as long as humans have existed, people have wanted to develop ways of remembering things. That's why they have written notes using cuneiform and hieroglyphics. Think about when you were in your middle school algebra class. You might have used an acronym to help you remember the correct order of operations, PEMDAS: Parentheses, Exponents, Multiplication, Division, Addition, and Subtraction. To make this concept clearer, your algebra teacher might have used the sentence, "Please Excuse My Dear Aunt Sally," which was perhaps nonsensical, but helped reinforce the concept. You probably still haven't forgotten that phrase. And it is highly likely that you would be able to solve a basic arithmetic problem based on this information alone. In addition to basic things like math, you can also use acronyms to remember a person's name and face. For example, take the case of a person named Jacob. You could construct the meaning for that person's name based on the characteristics you assign to that person.

    Joyful
    Agreeable
    Caring
    Obedient
    Brave

Each of these adjectives will describe a specific person of whom you are thinking, whether that is a good friend, classmate, or colleague. Using this acronym, you can remember this name with no problem. It can be better than any other method.

Creating a Memory Seating Chart

Teachers have the perennial anxiety of learning the names of their students each semester and year. Instructors working in multicultural environments might also find learning names to be a chore and difficult task. Not to worry! It is possible. Remembering the names of students in large classrooms might be a daunting task; however, it can be fun and enjoyable. One way teachers can remember where their students are is by creating a classroom seating chart, where they place each student on a chair in the room.

Then, in those virtual "chairs," you can do your grading for their participation and attendance. Using a seating chart helps teachers visualize where exactly the students are during class time. It can help a teacher learn names fast and creates a spatial dimension to the learning of names and faces.

In Different Cultures: Use English Names

English teachers working in China are known to give their students English names because they have trouble correctly pronouncing Chinese names. This method is handy for teachers working in Chinese universities, where they will teach anywhere from 120-150 students per week in their classes. It allows the teacher to build strong associations between names and faces. Also, whether you assign names yourself or allow your students to choose their names, in many cases those selections will connect to the unique personality of the student. As such, you will have an additional piece of information to help you associate the name with the right person. "He looks just like a Nathan."

Rhymes

Rhyming is another mnemonic device that has been used for hundreds of years. This method can help students memorize lists of hundreds of words. Shakespeare used rhymes in his work, as he wrote in blank verse and iambic pentameter to make his lines more memorable. Quoting authors like Shakespeare, Wordsworth, and Dickinson is possible for virtually any person because the rhyme scheme enables us to do so. Look at some examples of rhymes.

• In fourteen hundred and ninety-two, Columbus sailed the ocean blue.

• The highwayman came riding, riding, riding, the Redcoats looked to their priming… (Noyes, 1947)

• All's well that ends well.

• Red sky in the morning, shepherd's warning.

Poetry is often meant to be read aloud and therefore can be remembered through rhyming. The sound of similar end sounds of words enables people to remember the words of a poem or phrase. It also makes it much easier to recite poetry by heart.

How Do You Memorize a Poem for a Poetry Slam?

Have you ever wanted to know how people can memorize super-long poems? It does not happen by staring down at a page for hours on end. Instead, remembering a whole poem requires a person to visualize different aspects of the poem. When you learn a poem by heart, you take in all the sights and sounds of the poem fresh off the page. You use your senses to study poetry. Say you're learning a poem about fall. Then you can visualize the smell of crisp autumn leaves falling to the ground with colors of gold, orange, and red. You think about all those things and construct the images in your mind.

After studying the images, which you have visualized in your mind, then you can memorize the actual words of the poem. The strategy is not rote memorization. It is creating the image of the poem, so it is real to you. If you cannot clearly visualize what is in the poem, it will be tough to memorize it. You will remember one minute, and then the next, you will forget. Many people memorize this way and within moments, they forget everything. They look at a sheet and stare blankly into it, and then recall it for a test, where they can write down the answers. But once they turn in the test, it's done. They have forgotten everything they learned. It's as though the memory never seeped into their minds. It may have entered the short-term memory. But after that, it completely disappeared, because it never became a long-term memory.

Case Study

Jericho enjoyed reading poetry everywhere. He wanted to learn how to memorize the poems because he wanted to recite them at his school's poetry reading. He worked hard on memorizing "The Raven" by Edgar Allan Poe. This was one of his favorite middle school poems. And he wanted to challenge himself to remember the entire poem by recalling the onomatopoeic words that he spoke as he was practicing aloud. Here is an example of a section from the poem he was able to memorize perfectly:

Once upon a midnight dreary, while I pondered, weak and weary,

Over many a quaint and curious volume of forgotten lore —

While I nodded, nearly napping, suddenly there came a tapping,

As of someone gently rapping, rapping at my chamber door.

"'Tis some visitor," I muttered, "tapping at my chamber door —

Only this and nothing more."

As he memorized each line from this poem, he started to visualize the scene with the raven tapping at the narrator's chamber door. He was then able to recreate the image in his mind's eye, which helped him to see what was happening. Finally, he could speak the whole poem without seeing the words on the page. During the poetry reading, he recited the entire poem by heart, and the crowd went wild when they heard him do it.

Memorizing Lines for the Town Play

Have you ever wanted to know how actors can remember their lines so well? Think back to Linus's concern in *A Charlie Brown Christmas*: "I can't memorize these lines so quickly. Why do I have to be put through such agony?!" Like Linus, we may feel burdened by the thought of having to memorize things, but it is not too hard to do. Learning lines for a play or movie script can be done quickly and efficiently. But you need to use some mnemonic devices to do it well. Many times, actors will visualize the role they have to take on and then they act it out. It can be fascinating to watch them pull it off in front of many people. This technique helps actors to incarnate the role they are playing. Everything begins with reading the script, but then once you're on camera, you create the character, which creates a visual memory that helps the actor remember well. Essentially, it is a total body experience, so the actor can easily and fluidly recall all the lines from the script and embody the characters they were meant to play.

Case Study

Corinne was a drama queen — in a good way. She loved acting and doing various parts of the university drama. However, she didn't have a good memory. She would cram all the lines of the play into her mind.

Because she had a terrible memory, the directors didn't give her important parts in the play. Furthermore, she continually received the supporting roles and sometimes minor characters. It made Corinne feel bad. She needed to train intentionally to develop her memory, so she could get a key role in the next play.

Soon, Corinne started to use mnemonic devices to remember essential information from the play. She used them every day to remember the lines of the play. As soon as she had another audition, she knocked the socks off the director and his stage manager. Corinne was able to remember all the lines of her monologue clearly. It was an amazing day, as she felt confident she could recite her lines without any problem.

Creating a Memory Palace

The Ancient Greeks used a technique called the Memory Palace, an edifice of memory. This is another example of the method of loci that I mentioned at the beginning of this chapter. When you create a memory palace, you imagine that your memory is a large structure, which contains in its chambers the memories of different aspects of your life. Visualizing your palace of memory and its various spaces, each of which contains vital information, allows you to remember parts of your life more easily and efficiently. Imagine you are Socrates, and you are invited to give a TED talk. You must do your entire speech by heart and must use the technique that was first used by the Greeks. How can you do that? Let's create a memory palace together.

(Ideally, when you build your memory palace, you would close your eyes to help you focus and imagine. But since you need to read this book, keep your eyes open).

Imagine that you are standing in the driveway of your house. Look inside your door's window. Then, walk inside. You see Winnie the Pooh dancing with his friends in your living room. Turn left, and you see Anne Marie scantily dressed, dancing, and singing her song "2002" on your coffee table. You also see the Teenage Mutant Ninja Turtles walking down the hallway. Together, they are singing the "Ghostbusters" song. Then, you go into the kitchen where you see Martha Stewart cooking her Thanksgiving meal with turkey and stuffing. The smell is delicious. She is sautéing the garlic, onions, and vegetables for the different dishes. Then, you go to the bathroom, where you see Teletubbies singing and dancing. Finally, you come outside, and you see John Lennon singing "Imagine" in your backyard, with the sun setting in the background.

Now open your eyes. You probably cannot remember every single detail exactly as I told you. But with different bits of information, you will be able to piece everything together by walking through the memory palace. You will use your existing memory to assemble the different parts of the memory, so you can recall it on demand afterward. This is one of the key ways different people can remember lists of information, among many other things.

Military Method

Our minds cannot capture every detail of a scene. We don't have the photographic capacity. While some people have a better memory than others, our brains are not cameras. People who have extraordinary memory capacity are called "eidetikers," but even these people may forget key information and don't have a completely photographic memory ("Eidetic memory," n.d.). You might be saying to yourself, "I have a terrible memory. I cannot even remember my telephone number." While you might be discouraged, never fear. You can train your brain to remember the details of anything. One of the best ways to do this is to use the military method.

The military has done a fair amount of research and training in this area, including spies, objective viewing, and photographic memory (Boureston, n.d.). The American military has trained many soldiers to remember coordinates, maps, and many other things. We can definitely learn a lot from their findings. Let's use the military method to develop not only a good memory, but also a photographic one.

Disclaimer

Before we explain the military method, you should know that this method will take a while to develop. You cannot acquire it overnight. You should give yourself at least a month or two to complete this experiment. You must practice it every day. If you miss even one day, you'll have to start over. You must find time in your schedule to do this every day.

Adopting the Military Method

Let's now look at the steps to help you do the military method today (Boureston, n.d.).

Step 1:

Find a dark, windowless room where you can turn off all the lights. Find a place where you won't be distracted. However, you should have a bright light to shine overhead. A good place to do this would be a bathroom.

Step 2:

Sit in a position where you can quickly illuminate and darken the room without having to leave your seat. Find a sheet of paper and cut out a hole in the shape of a rectangle, about the size of a paragraph from a book you are reading.

Step 3:

Take the book or thing you're trying to memorize and cover it with the piece of paper, revealing only one paragraph from the text. Sit a reasonable distance from the book so that when you open and close your eyes, you can see and concentrate on memorizing the words readily.

Step 4:

Turn off the lights and let your eyes adjust to the darkness in the room. Turn the light on for a split second and then turn it off. By now, you will have the image of the text encoded into your memory with the information that was placed before your eyes.

Step 5:

If you find the memory of the text fading, turn the light on again for a split second and stare back at the text.

Step 6:

Keep doing this until you can remember all the words in the paragraph in order. If you do this step right now, you can create a visual in your mind and read the images of the text, as if it were right before your eyes. Your mind has imprinted these images in your mind like a photograph.

Practice doing this once a day for fifteen minutes for one month. You must commit to doing it every day for one month. If you do this, you will be able to recall information from any text you're trying to memorize. It will be fantastic.

As you train yourself to remember, you will visualize the different parts of the texts and apply the military method to your life. This will help you to master different bits of information and can help you as a student.

Case Study: Ron White, Two-Time USA Memory Champion

Ron White used five different military techniques to win a memory championship. He was coached by a former Navy SEAL, TC Cummings, who helped him to achieve his goal (Ron White Memory Expert, 2016). The training involved a lot of hard work. It was not easy. With his drive to win and unwavering dedication, White was successful in training his memory. Although White was not a Navy SEAL, he learned a lot from the training of military guys. Let's look at some highlights of what White did in this process.

1. "The more you sweat in times of peace, the less you bleed in times of war." (Ron White Memory Expert, 2016)

White knew he had to challenge himself, so he put himself to the test daily. When training for memory competitions or other matters of importance, you have to prepare your memory as if it is in wartime, instead of a relaxing time by the pool, because you might have to undergo a difficult moment in the competition. Our lives are not meant to be easy. We have to go through some difficult times that test us to the max. Furthermore, we must face near-death situations when we are in peacetime, so we can encounter the challenging moments of our lives.

To illustrate this point, White went underwater in cold weather in January with a deck of cards and scuba gear. In this situation, he memorized decks of cards while underwater. It was a torturously tricky task, but by training himself in this extreme way, he made the competition easier than his training. He faced the elements, and it prepared him better than if he were training under easy and normal conditions.

2. Develop a Winning Mindset

Secondly, if you want to be good at memorizing anything, you must have a winning mindset. Think about the Model United Nations competition that you won with the Best Delegate in Committee award. Recall how your friends and teachers cheered you on as you went up to the podium to receive your award. Get yourself pumped and ready to achieve all the things you want to do. Envision your success, whatever that looks like for you, and then live into it.

3. Start with Small and Gradual Goals

If you want to memorize a long poem or lines for a play, start a little bit at a time. Memorize a short selection of text each day. For example, Dean Peterson memorized a whole chapter of Moby Dick by creating a memory palace, but it required him to do it gradually, with hard work (2016).

As you go step-by-step, you will reach your target. But you have to put in the work because nothing happens overnight. Everything worth doing requires patience and dedication.

In religious circles, memorizing and meditating on different sacred texts is common practice. Give yourself a few verses to recall each day, and then you will see how quickly the text comes back to your memory upon recall.

4. Always Have Consequences for Not Reaching the Target

White said that we might have goals we want to achieve, but then we fall short in hitting our target. Losing is a consequence that can occur, but we must give ourselves some form of light punishment, such as taking a cold shower for three minutes, especially if we greatly dislike having cold water poured on us. It may be easy for us to shove it aside and not worry about it, but we need to find ways of having consequences in our lives for something we did not do properly. The more adjusted we are to consequences, the better off we will be in the long run.

5. Train Even When You Don't Feel Like Doing It

One crucial aspect of training for a competition or a test is that you have to train every day, even when you don't feel like it. You must develop the discipline to do it even on the days when you would rather be doing nothing at all. White had to face the music with this when he was training. He was feeling ill and told his trainer, Cummings, "TC, I'm sick. I cannot come in to train." TC told him he had to come in to train (Ron White Memory Expert, 2016). He had no choice. Just because he was sick didn't mean that he could skip his training.

On the day of the competition, White faced another terrible obstacle. He wasn't ill, but he had only gotten forty-five minutes of sleep the night before. Sleep deprivation could pose a big problem for most people. However, White had trained for this. He already knew the conditions because he had trained when he was feeling sick. He had spent months preparing for the memory competition, and he wasn't going to let that stand in the way of him getting the first prize. He went after it with all he had and then won the competition. It was an incredible result.

Person-Action-Object (PAO) System

The Person-Action-Object System is a method of memorizing that involves using numbers, people, action, and objects (Person-Action-Object (PAO) System, n.d.). In this method, the person thinks of a set of numbers and then assigns a person for each one of them. To remember the person, they can think of the different numbers and form associations with the people. Additionally, with this system, you can think of a person and action, such as Spiderman, who is spinning his web and flying from buildings. Then, to remember a number, you might assign him a random number. In the end, you form word associations and images that can help you remember a set of data or different objects. Such information can be used to recall playing cards, phone numbers, places, and people. It can be a very useful way of memorizing vital information.

Major Systems

Another technique that can help people remember better is major systems, which converts numbers into phonetic vowels and then into words and images. When you use this method, you can think of both sound words that associate the numbers with those sounds. And then, you can also use this information to connect it to a word. Then, you can use that word to produce an image in your head. It makes it a lot easier to remember the words, as well. You can use this information to memorize long lists of phone numbers, data, among many other items. It can also be quite helpful in your memorization efforts.

Mind Maps

The final method that can help you memorize is by creating a mind map. It is an idea in which you take a central theme and illustrate it using only keywords or phrases that you can connect to the central theme. You use short lines to connect everything to the central idea in the middle. The words attached to it are called associations, and they relate to the theme with all ideas connected to the idea. Mind maps are especially useful as graphic organizers that you can use to remember various pieces of information. Many people in this world are visually oriented. This method permits visual learners to thrive by putting down words on paper and organizing ideas that can be readily memorized and reproduced on a test or for other events in a person's life.

Last Thing: Practice, Practice, Practice!

To remember things well, you need to practice as much as possible. There is truth to the adage, "practice makes perfect." You will have to constantly repeat and do things over and over again for them to work out. You cannot allow your memory to go through periods of withdrawal without this practice. You need to frequently refresh your memory and muscle memory of the things you have learned, and that requires you to do things repeatedly. When you are studying for a test, preparing a lecture or speech, or planning something, you should practice in front of a mirror and do it as often as possible. Only then will you gain confidence and be able to handle any situation you are faced with.

Example

Danny was getting ready to do his presentation for a company, and he had written up his speech on PowerPoint slides. He knew that he would have to remember all the information and didn't want to look at his notes unless he ran into an emergency. Therefore, he tried with all his might to remember the details of his presentation. He went over it continually for several weeks. He timed it exactly so that it would never go over 20 minutes. When he arrived at his presentation, he was able to do it flawlessly, without referring to his notes, and his timing was almost perfect. It was all because he had taken the time to practice and practice some more.

PART II: DEVELOPING PHOTOGRAPHIC MEMORY SKILLS — THE BEGINNER'S GUIDE

CHAPTER 5: PHOTOGRAPHIC MEMORY

The human imagination is one of the greatest abilities on the planet. It has the power to create ideas, concepts and images that are out of this world. When you imagine things in your mind, the possibilities are nearly endless.

One of the most important ways we can remember something is by associating our memories with absurd images that may not line up with the actual memory itself. But it helps us remember better.

Think of the following associations, crying and squealing babies, sloshing through sheets of snow, barrels of butter, among others. These kinds of images use alliteration and other literary techniques to help you remember the image better. As we use our senses, we also use our imagination to help us remember things well.

Having a good imagination will help you to develop a photographic memory. If you want to do this, watch movies, read books, and incorporate other media that will aid in your memory.

Turn the Sounds of Names into Images

Let's give an example of how this all works.

Maybe you are learning the names of people in your life. You meet a man named Daniel, and you think to yourself, "I've completely forgotten the name of that man. How did that happen?" You could think of the Daniel in the lion's den from the Bible story or you could link the name to someone you have already met by that name.

As soon as you have formed these connections, you won't easily forget a name again. Another example is making an association with words. You might meet a girl named Jasmine, and you think to yourself, "Jasmine, how will I remember her name?" Maybe you like jazz, so you think of Duke Ellington playing a saxophone in a jazz concert. Then, the image sticks and you remember Jasmine's name and face.

It's that simple. Or, perhaps, you meet a guy named Charlie, and you think to yourself, "Charlie Chaplain? Charlie Brown?"

The more you associate names and images from cartoons or other media, the better your photographic memory will be.

Use Your Senses to Remember

As you're trying to memorize lists or numbers, try to use as many of your senses as possible. It helps you to memorize numerous things.

For example, you might know a man named Mike. You could visualize Mike singing with a microphone at a karaoke night, which helps you to remember effectively. Or, maybe you want to remember the name of a woman named Melanie, so you remember Melanie Hamilton, that "goody-goody" *from Gone with the* Wind, who was Scarlett O'Hara's rival and a woman who had a pure heart.

Use Sensory Memory to Re-Create Experiences

Many actors use sensory memory to re-create experiences as they are memorizing lines. For example, if they want to create an emotional scene where they are crying over a dead body, they might remember when they were mourning the loss of a loved one. Or, if they are mourning the loss of a girlfriend, they might recall a time in the past when they had broken up with someone. Then, they can effectively re-create the scene emotionally and physically.

If an actor needs to recreate the experience of a break-up, he can go back to the memory of a past break-up with his girlfriend in a restaurant. He can clearly visualize the garlic bread, salad with vinaigrette dressing, the candlelight in the middle of the table, and the pain in the stomach following the meal. By making all these associations with memories, he can emotionally prepare himself to act and incarnate his role.

CHAPTER 6: REMEMBERING NUMBERS

Numbers can often be difficult to remember. As hard as we try, it is challenging for us to remember basic phone numbers. Often, we revert to using our phones as an external memory device for all the figures we may have in our lives. We might think to ourselves, "My memory is not good. How in the world am I going to be able to remember all these numbers?" However, we can apply the same principles for memory enhancement to numbers. We can associate images with numbers. For example, you might have "0" and might think of a donut hole. Or, you might have the number 007, and you can instantly think of James Bond, who is associated with that number.

Many people can also remember names, because they had important significance, including 9/11 for September 11th or May 4th (May the Fourth be With You). With numbers, you can incorporate creativity to help you remember them.

Remember Numbers by Association

We remember things a lot better when we can associate them with different items. It is much harder to remember something based on arbitrary connections, but when you connect ideas, then you can recall long lists of numbers (Memorizing Dates and Numbers, Mnemonic Tricks, n.d.).

One way to quickly remember is by remembering the consonant system, which will help you associate each digit with a consonant based on different relationships.

For example:

0 – Z or S (Zero begins with the letter Z)

1 – T or D (You can see that T has a downward stroke and down starts with D)

2 – N (Capital N when rotated 90 degrees will look like a number 2)

3 – M (Capital M when rotated 90 degrees will look like the number 3)

4 – R (Capital R also looks like a backward 4. Also, it is the last letter of the word, four

5 – L (The Roman numeral for 50 is L)

6 – G (When you close the G, you can form the number 6)

7 – K (Capital K contains two sevens that mirror one another) C – The number 7 is also known as the complete number.

8 – F or B (When you write out a cursive F, it will look like 8. Likewise, the letter B looks like an 8.

9 – P (When you make a backward P it looks like 9)

You can associate any of these numbers with a consonant. You should memorize the letter that goes with each of those digits. Let's see how this works in practice.

Suppose you have to memorize the year that the Declaration of Independence was signed in 1776. To do this, you should substitute the numbers for the letters. In this case, you would have 1776: DCKG

DCKG by itself does not make any sense, so you have to add some vowels to make it work. You could write out Doc+King. It sounds like the word docking. You could imagine the settlers arriving in America, settling their land of independence from Britain. You could also think of it as the document ("Doc") that would liberate the colonies from the King of England. Now, you would be able to remember this figure much better. By making these real-life associations, you could recall the date 1776 instantly.

Make Words and Phrases from Phone Numbers

You can also make some words and phrases from the different phone numbers you have.

For example, 31415936: MTRTLPMG – My turtle named Pomegranate.

You can make all sorts of associations, which are fun and lively.

Case Study

Frank was not good at math or numbers. He forgot his passcode to his apartment and his phone number. Although he stored all the information in his phone, he still forgot the basic numerical information. As he was studying for exams as a student, he would forget the formulas and numbers he had learned right before because he relied on faulty rote memorization to get him through. Realizing his memory was not working well, he started to come up with ideas on how he could remember things better and more effectively. He started to remember numbers like 7, which could be associated with *7th Heaven*, the TV show. Or, he might remember 6 and link it to the Greek ideal of perfection. Then, he could remember a sequence, such as 747, by connecting it to a 747 airplane. By assembling these kinds of images in his mind, he could effectively recall different series of numbers. By linking all the numbers with patterns and images, he could remember figures and numbers.

CHAPTER 7: REMEMBERING ANNIVERSARIES AND DATES

Who hasn't forgotten a birthday or anniversary? We're always doing it, and we feel ashamed when it happens. There are some ways you can remember dates, using the same principles you use for numbers and figures. And you can apply them directly to the dates that are important to you.

Write the Important Dates Down in a Calendar

Men are especially prone to forgetting important dates, such as anniversaries. They generally have a pretty bad memory. Women can easily forget dates, too. What is the solution to these things? Write it down in your calendar. Having a physical calendar that you can write in with a pen is one of the surefire ways you can remember. There is something about the physical act of putting a pencil or pen to paper that etches the memory into our minds for a long time. You can also remember where you were when you wrote it down, which aids in remembering an event. You can then check it later when you need to have a refresher.

Get Your Calendar in Your Phone and Put Important Dates into It

Next, if your physical calendar is not readily available, you should get a calendar for your phone and put important dates into it. Many phones are equipped to handle large amounts of data. The least you can do is enter the dates that you need to remember. It will help so much. There is no excuse for forgetting once you have done that.

Set up Your Phone or Mobile Device to Remember for You

After you have put the important dates into your phone, you can have your phone send you notifications and reminders, which can happen the day before or even thirty minutes before an event is supposed to happen. There is genuinely no excuse for you to forget an important event or date.

Associate the Date with an Important Occasion

If you want to remember things on your own, you should try to associate this date with a momentous occasion. Remember the date that you had with your girlfriend or boyfriend. It was Valentine's Day in 2009. You both were in a restaurant eating Asian food. You can recall the smells of ginger, onion, and garlic, the colorful artwork on the walls, the steam curling up from the tea, and the simple, stringed music playing in the background. As you associate all these images with your special time, you will not easily forget what happened. You can then link these ideas to your date, and you will remember it forever.

Look at Photos from Your Anniversary Dinners

Another thing you can do to prep yourself for remembering important dates, such as anniversaries, is to look at photos. Recall photos from your anniversary, wedding, or other important occasions. When you put those images in your mind, then you will easily make them memorable. Fortunately for us, we have photos that help bring back memories. We must take many of them throughout our lives to help bring back the memory. It will help you recall that important date.

CHAPTER 8: REMEMBERING INFORMATION

Recalling information is something we need to learn how to develop as we go throughout our lives. There are different ways we can remember key information. Let's look at the ways we can remember different bits of vital information

Chunking

Chunking is a way of memorizing something that involves grouping items together in a list and recalling things in small chunks. For example, you might have a list of numbers and you have to remember the whole list. Instead of recalling each number one by one, you can try to memorize the information in groups.

For example, say the phone number you're trying to learn goes something like (433) 867-3135, you can memorize each part in chunks. You can start with 433 and then move on to

867 and so on. Reciting numbers from memory often involves grouping them, which helps you when you have to recall instantly and cannot readily reach for your phone, which has the information carefully stored inside it (Lickerman, 2009).

Writing Down the Information Over and Over

Another great way you can consolidate information is by writing something over and over again in your notebook. This method seems to work with students who need to memorize vocabulary words. They can write it several times at home, and once they have done that, then they can remember the words clearly and effectively.

You can recall memorized words faster when you have physically written them down in a notebook. Then, your mind can form the mental image needed to reproduce it on a test or quiz.

Make Meaning of the Words That You Are Memorizing

Rote memorization is not a useful tool for helping students memorize information. It is something that many Asian schools are proud to do. Especially in countries like China and Korea, many students are used to rote memorization of facts and figures. However, this method has proven to be ineffective for the overall retention of information. Instead, it is something for which students use their working memory that lasts from a few minutes to hours and not long-term memory, which is consolidated in the brain. Therefore, there are many cram schools open to help students memorize and study a significant amount of material in a short period of time, but students are not genuinely learning from this experience. Rather than memorizing words without a context, you should find ways to make sense of all the words you are trying to remember. Don't merely stare at words on a page. Make meaning out of them. Create word associations and analogies that will piece them together and make them easier to remember. It will change your life.

When Studying for Tests, Summarize Information

One key method for studying for tests involving memorization of texts or information is summarizing. When you are studying, you can create summaries of the information you need to recall for a test or quiz. By putting things in your own words, you can effectively re-create the ideas and concepts in a way that makes sense to you. Then, you demonstrate your true knowledge of the subject. It is not enough to memorize vital information. If you genuinely internalize and process it, then it will be easier for you to recall and store the information. When you need to recall it, such as in an exam situation, you will be able to remember and reproduce it in written or spoken form. This helps you to remember details, such as speeches or other things.

When Studying for Something, Study in the Afternoon

While most people can be either a morning or evening person, it has been shown that most people are often alert in the afternoon (Lickerman, 2009). This is because we are completely awake and have had our meals and coffee for the day. Then, we can focus and concentrate on the tasks at hand. For some people, the morning is a good time to study or get work done. However, the afternoon is when we are completely awake. If you are studying for a test, try to do most of it during the afternoon from 1-4. Then, you shouldn't have trouble with remembering. You can rest in the evening and allow your brain to recall different experiences.

CHAPTER 9: FOREIGN LANGUAGE LEARNING — MEMORIZING KEY WORDS

Foreign language learning has never been easier than today. It is continually advancing and allowing students to learn at a faster rate than before. Different countries have developed unique approaches to teaching foreign languages. Some are useful, and others are ineffective. But each one has its own strength in helping students remember words. Let's look at some of the basics of foreign language learning that enable you to memorize and consolidate key information.

Grammar-Translation Method

The grammar-translation method is used in Korea, China, Japan, and many other Asian countries. It has been used for generations to help students develop their foreign language competence. The principle is translating every concept, idea, sentence, paragraph, and structure from the target language into the source language. The key words in the foreign language are directly translated into the first language of the learner. With this method, the learner will memorize essential vocabulary in two languages, as well as fundamental sentences that are translated into the person's first language. Within this bilingual context, the student picks up on crucial information by referring back to their first language. Using this background knowledge helps the student to develop fluency in the target language. However, with constant translation back and forth, this method may not be effective.

In many cases, students rely on rote memorization. In schools in Korea, for example, students might be given a list of 100 words and asked to memorize the entire list. Then, they might have to reproduce it on an exam the next day. This forces them to cram every day for word tests. However, it is not proven to enable students to recall the information. Instead, it is something that just superficially fills the need to acquire a language.

There are, however, merits for using the grammar-translation method. For one, it can help students develop their reading proficiency. When students have access to their background knowledge in their first language, it makes it easier for them to read in the second language. For example, you might have a student reading *Hamlet* in Korean or Chinese. They can use this background knowledge to read the same text in English confidently. Then they shouldn't have too many problems with encountering the text in the target language. There might be some concepts or ideas that need a dictionary or pocket translator. For the most part, though, they can access the information directly from the translated version, which helps in comprehension.

Spaced Repetition: Flashcards

A tried and tested method of learning a foreign language includes spaced repetition. Many people use flashcards to help them remember a concept or idea. Repetition is needed to consolidate information in our heads for the long-term. We cannot constantly rely on our working memory for key details. Instead, if we want to remember everything from a list, we must rely on our long-term memory. That includes taking steps to recall words. When you are memorizing words, you can use flashcards, apps like Studyblue and Cram.com, among other tools. Spaced repetition enables you to remember things clearly, because you do it over and over again until it becomes etched into your memory.

Analogies and Word Families

When memorizing words, it is often a good idea to make connections with the words. For example, you can use analogies and word families to connect ideas. Take for example, the word fraternal. It means "brother." You can try to find all the words that are related to this word. For example, you have fraternal, fraternity, fraternization, among others. Then, you can connect all these ideas to family and brother. Once you have made this connection, then you will be able to remember the word more effectively.

Another example is masculine. You can find the list of other related words and connect the ideas. For example, you might think of male, masculine, masculinity, masculinization, among others. All of these words are related to the word "male." As a result, you can easily connect the ideas and memorize the words. This also enables you to remember not just one word but many words because you can chunk the ideas together. Another example is female. You can connect this idea to feminine, feminization, femininity, feminism, and other words. Then, you can memorize all these words because they are in the same word family.

Voice Recording of Words

Another way that you can memorize words is by recording your voice. This is a proven method to help you remember. First, you can write down a list of words that you want to memorize multiple times in your notebook, and then you can speak out them to your voice recorder. Then, you can easily recall the information because you have used your senses to remember. You should also do this contextually, which means reading not just words, but also passages and sentences that include key words. Then, you can mentally create pictures of the words you need to memorize.

Word Pictures

One common method of memorizing words includes making word pictures. For example, say you have a list of words that are unrelated to one another. You can visualize each word on the page and connect them, which enables you to memorize the whole list of words. When you can think of an image for each word and then connect them with a story, then you will be able to recall the information. This can help you with a quiz, especially if the quiz has the same word order. However, if you don't have the same order, it can prove to be a challenging method of memorization.

Use Your Latin and Greek Roots

In addition to word pictures and associations, you should also use your Greek and Latin roots. English includes words that are related to Greek and Latin. Likewise, languages such as French, Italian, and Spanish have words that are related to Latin. They are called Romance languages. When you learn these popular foreign languages, you can remember a lot better when you connect the ideas to a Latin root. For example, the word "magnificent" is related to the word "magnifique" in French. You can also relate it to the word "magnify," which means to make larger. This comes from the Latin root magn-, which means "great." Making these connections and relating the terms you learn to both Latin roots and English words will be valuable.

Learn Words within a Context

Another key aspect of language learning is acquiring a foreign language within a context. No language exists in a vacuum. You cannot rely on your memorization skills to remember words that are disconnected and unrelated to each other. You need to have a context and word web that brings together even unrelated words. Then, you can effectively remember multiple pieces of information. You don't recall the word in question, but also you remember all the different words that connect that idea. Contextual memorization is an integral part of language development. For example, say you are learning to read a story in a foreign language. You can memorize key sentences from that story, which helps you remember the ideas, the pronunciation, and spelling of those sentences. When you have to recall that information on a test or in a presentation, you can instantly remember the words to the story. It shows that you have genuinely mastered the material.

Case Study

Jasmine was a good language learner. She wanted to commit more things to memory. She studied French for a long time. All through school, students and teachers had told her, "Jasmine, you need to memorize 100 words a day and take word tests all the time and know the translation from French to English." But then, everyone else did terrible when they spoke French out loud. Instead of going this route, Jasmine read a lot in French. She would read a bunch at home and try to do her best to see French within a written context. It helped a lot. She also did her word memorization through spaced repetition, which enabled her to reach a high level in French.

What helped Jasmine remember better was how she associated English words with French words through different roots. It helped her remember them better. Additionally, she would make word pictures with all the things she tried to memorize. She would visualize the word and then draw a picture, which helped her to capture the memory of it better. Jasmine worked on learning different words and translations. She used a dictionary and would create thousands of word pictures. It was an effective way to remember.

What's more, Jasmine went to France for seven weeks to do an immersion program in French. In that program, she was only allowed to speak French the whole time. Nothing else. It would prove to be an intense challenge for her, but at the end of the time, she was speaking French like a pro. It was amazing!

After that time, Jasmine did not have a lot of practice with French. Sometimes, she would practice it with friends and French people she met. However, she was not given a lot of opportunities to speak it. On the other hand, whenever she spoke it, the words came out effortlessly as if she had not forgotten it. Although she was not practicing, Jasmine could clearly remember how to speak French, and she could activate it whenever she wanted to do that. It was a fantastic testament to the fact that she had mastered a foreign language. That she was able to speak French fluently even without practice proved that she had successfully put the foreign language in her permanent memory bank. That is the benefit of being bilingual. It's a gift and a talent.

CHAPTER 10: HIGH-SPEED MEMORY TIPS

Let's now look at some ways you can beef up your memory. In addition to the ability to acquire foreign languages, your brain has a high capacity to remember things at an amazing capacity and speed. Here are some tips that will help you get into the right place.

Stay Hydrated

One of the most important things we can do for our memories is to drink enough water. This point cannot be stressed enough. You need to drink plenty of fluids throughout your day. Otherwise, you will get dehydrated. The majority of the body is filled with water, so we have to find ways to hydrate ourselves throughout the day. Otherwise, we won't be as sharp as we want to be. Drink at least 2-3 liters of water per day. Your body and mind will feel the difference.

Drink Coffee or Tea: Caffeine Works Wonders

Many people drink caffeine to get their day started. It has proven benefits and can help us to be more energetic. In fact, drinking more coffee can help our digestive system and increase our memory because we can activate those neurons in our brains responsible for memory consolidation. In case you feel guilty about your addiction to caffeine or coffee, never fear. It will be helpful to your overall feeling and help you remember things a lot better. Not to mention, a jolt of caffeine every day will help you to concentrate on your important tasks. So, get you a cup of hot Americano from "Starbies." You will feel the difference in mind and in body.

Try to Teach Someone Else What You Have Learned

It is no secret that the way to remember something is to teach others how to do it. You need to be able to explain in your own words a concept or idea. When you do this, your memory recall will be faster and more efficient. Find ways you can recycle your ideas. Hash it out with your friend and do a workshop on it. You will have a faster recall, and it will help you to master the content.

Think While You Walk and Talk

One efficient way to learn something effectively is by multitasking and doing something else while you're trying to master something. For example, when you walk and talk, you can effectively externalize your thoughts and also activate your memory, which takes in these experiences. It helps you to remember things much better. If you want to talk it out, you have to walk the walk. It is effective.

Study in a Stimulating and Low-Key Environment

When you are studying for a test or something else, find an environment that suits you. Whether that is in a library, at home in your living room, or at a coffee shop, find something that floats your boat. Often, it is in the low-key and stimulating environments where we can find our sweet spot for studying. Know what's right for you and do it. This will greatly help your concentration power and give you the skill needed to ace the tests you might have or remember things faster.

Play Instrumental Music While You Work or Study

Another method that may help your concentration and boost your memory power is playing low-key instrumental music no faster than 60 beats per minute. When you listen to music that has a lot of lyrics or instruments, it might distract you rather than help you. Find some study or concentration music on YouTube. There are plenty of choices, and you won't be disappointed. Find music that is meaningful to you and make it into your work or study jam. You will be able to be more effective in your memorization game.

Relax

Finally, you should find ways to relax because we often don't remember things well when we are tense or stressed. Find ways to live your life in a balanced and low-key way. Stay away from too much tension. Allow your stress to melt away. Relax, because life is short. And if you want to remember more effectively and faster, you should find ways to take a load off. Do it today, for your memory's sake.

CHAPTER 11: MEMORIZING GAME CARDS

One of the key ways we can use memory is by remembering game cards. This is a technique that is often employed by poker players or casino dealers at Las Vegas. An essential aspect of remembering cards is through making word associations with images. When you can remember a number, you can put an image to it and easily remember it, which will help you when you're playing the game with others. Let's look at some tricks you can use when you're memorizing playing cards.

Using Peg Words

One important way to remember cards is by using peg words, such as H2 for hen, which has two hearts, H3 for ham, which has three hearts, and H4 for hair, which has four hearts. When you can assign a word to the card or number, it will help you remember much better. Let's look at the basics of pegs in a card game (How to Count Cards, n.d.).

1: Spade has one point

2: Heart, which has two halves

3: Club has three leaves

4: Diamond has four points

You can use each of these numbers for the different suits and then you can memorize each card associated with that suit. For example, if you have a diamond that has 1, you might associate it with 401, and then you can make the association with that, as you're memorizing the cards. Instead of saying 1 of diamonds, you can use this number, which it makes it a lot easier to recall (How to Count Cards, n.d.).

Take an Imaginary Walk Somewhere

You will take a walk through a familiar place, like your home or an office building. As you do a walk through this place, you will become intimately familiar with 52 spots that you can apply to your mental journal (How to Memorize A Deck of Cards, 2019). Then, choose 5 rooms where you want to store the information. For example, you could choose your bedroom, bathroom, kitchen, or home office.

In each of the five rooms, memorize 10 items of furniture. Imagine you've stepped into the place and you scout out the 10 furniture items. Then, look at them clockwise in your memory. Move around in the room and visualize each item.

Then, repeat all these items in your head repeatedly. Try to lock in these items in your memory by repeating as much as possible (How to Memorize A Deck of Cards, 2019).

Finally, add two pieces of furniture that will complete the 52 cards.

Make the 52 Cards into 52 Famous People

You will remember cards more vividly when you assign a picture to them. Why not try imagining 52 celebrities and matching them to the 52 cards? This will make memorization much easier (How to Memorize A Deck of Cards, 2019).

Find Ways of Remembering Each Card

Now, think of a way you can remember each card by looking at each card as if it were male or female. For example, kings are male and are half of a celebrity couple. And queens are the female half of the couple. Jacks are male and they are bachelors. So, you could say that Jacks are famous male bachelors (How to Memorize A Deck of Cards, 2019).

The highest numbers in the deck are 10 and 9. They represent powerful people. 10 is the most famous woman. And 9 is the most powerful man.

Number 8 looks like an hourglass and can resemble a body. Therefore, 8 and 9 represent the body of the man and woman. For example, 8 represents a woman with a fabulous physique and 9 is a man who has a great body.

Number 5 and 6 sound like fight and sex, so this couple will be controversial. 6 will represent a woman who is controversial and 5 is a controversial man.

Now, think of the number of actors or actresses who have starred in a famous trilogy.

Number 4 will be the number of women who have starred in a trilogy and 3 will be the men who have been in a trilogy. Imagine those in your mind.

Number 1 is also known as Ace, which is a tennis term. For these, you can think of 1 and 2 as the top athletes in a sport.

CHAPTER 12: TRICKS TO IMPROVE READING SPEED

Many people want to learn how to speed up their memory. They also want to improve their reading speed. How do we go about doing that? This chapter will explain the ins and outs of improving your reading speed and how you can be a better reader.

Stop the Inner Monologue

Growing up, we probably found ourselves in a classroom where our teacher taught us how to read by sounding out the words on a page and pronouncing them. Many people continue to sound out words as they are reading them on a page. While this habit is instinctively formed while we are in grade school, some people still do it even in their adult years, and it is not necessary. You can stop yourself from reading aloud and read the words on a page while looking at it. Instead of speaking to yourself, you can silently pronounce the words to yourself, which will help you to do it faster (Bullard, n.d.).

Chunking

Another strategy that is essential for reading faster is chunking. This technique allows you to read multiple words at the same time. When you group the words on a page, then your brain can process the information simultaneously, which makes it easier to read something. Often, we find ourselves staring at the same page and looking at similar words over and over. Sometimes, we read things multiple times for understanding. But we can improve our reading ability if we chunk ideas together and piece them like a puzzle (Bullard, n.d.).

Use Your Peripheral Vision

Many times, we might be using our tunnel vision and staring at each word on the page. To increase our reading speed, we should try to use our peripheral vision, which also helps us to take in words on a page. We can then process whole sentences rather than going word by word. This increases our capacity to read a book or article. It also helps us to comprehend what we are reading more effectively.

Use a Timer

Set a timer on your phone, which will help train you to develop a faster reading speed. If you want to read two pages in one minute, you can set a timer for one minute. Then, you can race against time and increase your reading ability. This will help you to work on reading faster over time.

Paraphrase

As you're going through paragraphs on a page, it is important to learn how to paraphrase and summarize key sentences. Sometimes, we don't even need to read the entire sentence to understand the concept behind the words. When you use your paraphrasing and summarizing skills, you can immediately process the information and comprehend it since you have experience with the topic and can relate it to your life.

Use a Highlighter or Marker

To promote active reading, you can highlight or underline the text. Find the key words and underline them. Then, you can come back to them later when you study them. Sometimes, it takes looking at the words on the page and putting your pen or highlighter down to keep track of where you are on the page. Plus, when you have to come back to the material, you will know where you stopped.

Skim Paragraphs on Tests

A key technique that is used by test prep companies is skimming paragraphs for the main idea. Whenever you are doing a reading test for the TOEFL, SAT, or GRE, you can speedread a passage and remove each paragraph for the main idea. Sometimes, that includes browsing through the information and processing the information. For example, if you have a passage that has five paragraphs, you can read the first sentence of each paragraph and understand what each section is about. Then, when you go to the questions, you can delve in deeper into the topic and comprehend the passage as a whole. This technique helps you to get a lot done faster and enables you to ace the test.

Read More

Finally, one of the ways that you can develop your literacy skill is by reading more. That means you should read every text you can get your hands on. It can be a book, article, journal, magazine, newspaper, or any other kind of text. Practice reading a little bit every day. The more you practice, the better you will get at reading. Literacy is a skill that is to be mastered over the long-term. It takes lifelong learning to become a master at it, but you can begin to get good at it when you are young. That is why initiatives such as "Accelerated Reader" have helped millions of children get into the habit of reading because it helps them to develop and grow in their reading skill (Bullard, n.d.).

Case Study

Timothy was an avid reader. He would read books a lot during his free time. Whenever he was busy, he would still find time to read, which enabled him to master a lot of material.

What made him a talented reader was the fact that people had instilled a love for reading in him. His parents and teachers encouraged him to read from a young age, which inevitably led him to learn a lot more. Therefore, Timothy became a better reader. He could read a lot faster than other students. In the end, he was able to do better on standardized tests and various subjects he had to study in school. Timothy also graduated valedictorian from his school in Westminster, MA. He would go on to study history at Harvard University. It was a success story.

PART III: MEMORY FOODS & MEMORY ACTION PLAN

CHAPTER 13: THE BEST FOODS TO HELP YOU PREVENT ALZHEIMER'S DISEASE AND DEMENTIA

The risk of Alzheimer's disease has never been greater than now. Due to lifestyles that have not been helpful, many people are faced with the possibility that they will lose their memories later in life. Not to fear, though. You can enhance your memory by eating the right foods. It has been shown that food is an essential part of developing your memory, and you should follow a healthy diet.

The key to preventing dementia is to eat a certain amount of the recommended foods as often as you can. You should not overeat red meat, processed foods, or bakery goods. Here are foods that are sure to help you in the process of preventing memory loss (Rosenbloom, 2018).

1. Dairy

Dairy products have many proven health benefits because they have lactic acid bacteria and fatty acids, which are produced during fermentation. Recent studies have noted the effects that these fermented dairy products can have on a person's ability to function cognitively. In short, foods like fermented cheese and yogurt can help a person prevent Alzheimer's disease and dementia. Crichton et al. (2010) have shown that people who consume low-fat dairy products, such as yogurt and cheese, once a week can improve their brain's basic functions more than a person who does not (Ano and Nakayama, 2018).

2. Raw Leafy Greens

Greens, including spinach, kale, and romaine contain antioxidants and vitamin K. You should try to consume one cup of them every day.

3. Cruciferous Vegetables

Vegetables, like broccoli, cauliflower, and Brussels sprouts contain a high quantity of vitamin K and glucosinolates, which have antioxidants. To have the full effect, include three ½-cup servings in your meals during the week.

4. Blueberries

Many berries are helpful to the brain's function, and blueberries seem to have the most positive effects. They have flavonoids, which help the brain's pathways and mitigate the effects of aging. To improve your memory, eat ½ cup of any type of berries at least three times per week.

5. Beans

Currently, studies have been inconclusive as to why beans can be good for brain health, but it is possible that it is due to the number of antioxidants, fiber, and vitamins in them. To help you experience the effects, eat them instead of consuming red meat twice per week.

6. Nuts

Unsalted nuts contain a high content of antioxidants. In particular, walnuts have a lot of omega-3 fatty acid, which helps the brain. Try to eat ¼ cup of nuts each day.

7. Fish

All types of fish contain iodine and iron, which foster steady cognitive function. Fish, like salmon and trout, have omega-3 fatty acids, which boost brain activity. Eat them once per week.

8. Whole Grains

Add oats, brown rice, and whole-grain wheat bread to your diet, which will also help you to have a healthier diet.

9. Chicken

Chicken is a good substitute for processed meat, but you should only take in one serving in a day.

10. Olive Oil

For cooking, stick to olive oil as your main oil. Add it to your salad dressing. It has monounsaturated fats, vitamin E, and antioxidants.

11. Coffee and Caffeine (Heerema, 2019)

Caffeine in coffee has been associated with boosts in brain function and also prevents a person from experiencing a cognitive decline from dementia.

In addition, caffeine has been shown to improve memory, spatial memory, and working memory, which helps you experience a richer and healthier life.

Mediterranean Diet

In general, the Mediterranean diet has been shown to improve a person's ability to prevent themselves from getting dementia or cognitive decline. Therefore, it can significantly help a person to improve their overall health.

It is important to have a healthy lifestyle in addition to a healthy diet. Avoiding smoking and excessive drinking can help a person get on the right track. Risk factors for developing Alzheimer's disease include diabetes, high blood pressure, and obesity.

CHAPTER 14: A BRAIN-ENHANCING AND MEMORY IMPROVEMENT MENU

If you are looking to improve your cognitive function and have felt a bit foggy recently, then you may want to add brain-healthy foods to your diet. To help, let's look at the following one-day meal plan (Power Up: One Day Brain Boosting Meal Plan).

Food is medicine. If you want to gain energy and momentum, you should choose foods that are high in protein, vitamins, and minerals. When you are feeding your mind with good foods, make sure to add antioxidants, omega-3s, and vitamins because these will enhance your memory, lower your blood pressure, and help you to sharpen your mental skills.

Breakfast: Bowl of Oatmeal or Whole Grain Cereal with Berries

Breakfast has often been considered the most important meal of our day. It begins your metabolism, improves your mood, and helps with cognitive function. Oatmeal or whole grain cereal are great for your brain and help satiate your appetite for several hours. Carbs in the oats of oatmeal make glucose, which is your brain's primary fuel. Fiber will also help control your blood sugar and maintain a steady level.

To make this meal more interesting, you can add a variety of different toppings, such as blueberries, pomegranate seeds, Swiss cheese, brown sugar, and other things filled with nutrients.

Mid-morning Snack: Blueberries

When you snack two to three times a day, you can regulate your metabolism and avoid getting hungry throughout the day. It also helps your blood sugar not to go down, which could decrease your brain's function. However, you should be mindful by snacking on the right kinds of foods, such as fruits, vegetables, nuts, and protein foods.

A right type of food that fits the bill is blueberries, which are filled with antioxidants and other nutrients that help your spatial memory. Put blueberries on your cereal, yogurt, or even create a smoothie for the results.

Lunch: Salad

Lunch is a critical moment for you to energize your brain. You should begin your lunch by taking some deep breaths to reduce stress and then enjoy a healthy salad that has lots of vegetables, shredded cheese, hard-boiled eggs, and nuts.

You should include some leafy greens that have a lot of vitamin K. Add cheese, which contains vitamin B12. You can add some vegetables with bright colors, such as green peppers, tomatoes, and broccoli, which have omega-3 fatty acids.

Finally, pour on some olive oil or a balsamic vinaigrette to give your brain a good dose of monounsaturated fats.

Afternoon Snack: Green Tea and Toast

One way you can prevent yourself from tanking in the middle of the afternoon is by adding some almond butter to a slice of toast. You can also have celery sticks and some hot green tea.

Nuts contain a high amount of vitamin E, which can help with cognitive function and green tea contains the acid L-theanine, which promotes feel-good chemicals in the brain. The caffeine in the tea also helps with brain activity.

Dinner: Salmon with Lemon and Grilled Vegetables

Dinner is an important meal, because you are wrapping up the day, and you can enjoy time with friends or family, or spend your alone time with your favorite meal. One dish that is sure to please is salmon. It only requires 30 minutes to prepare, but it has memory-enhancing nutrients, including DHA and omega-3. If you add it to your diet twice a week, it can help reduce the risk of heart attack and stroke.

Dessert: Dark Chocolate

Everyone has some form of sweet tooth, which means that dessert can be an indispensable part of our diet. After dinner, we can relish the sweet foods that bring us joy and boost our mood. Why not try some dark chocolate after your meal? You can add it to a glass of warm milk and enjoy the antioxidants that help improve your alertness and make you feel better.

When you eat dark chocolate, you will feel good afterward, but you should be careful not to overdo it. Eat in moderation!

CHAPTER 15: MEMORY IMPROVEMENT ACTION PLAN FOR TWO WEEKS

Now that we have arrived at the action plan, we can go through all the ways to enhance your memory. In what follows, I will give you a 14-day action plan, which will tell you all the things you need to do to make progress.

Rate Your Current Mental and Physical Level

The first thing you should do before any memory improvement action plan is to rate your current memory level. You should assess both your objective and subjective memory levels because then you can find out what level you want to attain after this training. It is vital to gauge where we are and think about where we want to go. There are two factors you need to measure. The first is your subjective memory perception. This is what you perceive your memory to be. You rate your overall memory and then you talk about the things that you have trouble remembering, such as names, faces, and appointments, among other reasons. You also talk about when you lose track of your thoughts in conversation or in speeches, as well as having trouble remembering what you read from a book.

All of these examples point to your subjective memory, or what you think personally about your memory. To assess your objective memory, we can use a list of words that you will try to recall after looking at them and then doing something else. For example, say you look at the following list:

Trombone
Balloon
CD
Apartment
Blueberry
Baby
Sail
Cameleon
Professor
Stove

You look at this for two minutes and then take a twenty-minute break and do something else like read a newspaper, watch a TV show, or something else to distract yourself from the word list. Then, after the twenty minutes are over, you come back to a blank piece of paper and write down all the words you can remember. If you can remember at least eight of the words from this list, you will find that the 14-day

Memory Training program will be a piece of cake and that you will be able to master it in no time. However, if you got fewer than eight words correct, then you may see some massive improvement in your overall ability following these two weeks (Small, 2005).

Rate Your Physical Fitness

After completing your memory level test, you can then do a subjective assessment of your fitness level. In it, you can talk about the things you experience on a regular basis like insomnia, shortness of breath, rapid heart rate, impatience, worry or anxiety, among other things. You can also talk about your weight and height and gauge where you are on the scale (Small, 2005).

Now let's move on to the different days and what you should expect from your plan to enhance your memory.

First Monday, Day One

Breakfast

Drink a nice cup of Joe. Drink a 250mL cup of hot coffee black with no sugar or any additive. It will have the most nutrients and help you get through the day.

Eat a bowl of whole grain cereal with raspberries that will get you going in the morning.

Mid-Morning Exercise

Write your name using both your left hand and right hand. Then, use two pencils, one with your right hand and left hand at the same time.

Lunch

For lunch, eat a tuna salad sandwich with green leaf lettuce and mustard sauce. Then, eat a sliced apple. For a drink, have a glass of Earl Grey tea with lemon.

Stress Relief in the Afternoon

Find a mat or a comfortable place on the floor and lie down or sit comfortably. Breathe in deeply and exhale slowly.

Continue deep breathing exercises for one to two minutes, which will help you breathe away all the stress you may be experiencing.

Stress causes memory problems. Therefore, we need to find ways to get rid of it.

Afternoon Snack

Have a cup of tomato juice or soup, then eat a handful of unsalted walnuts. Drink a glass of iced tea or water with lemon.

Afternoon Mental Exercise

On a sheet of paper, write down two details you remember from your commute to work in the morning. As you return home or when you follow the same route tomorrow, look at this sheet of paper to see how you did.

Dinner

For dinner, have a green salad with chicken and balsamic vinaigrette and olive oil. Have a cup of brown rice and steamed spinach.

For a drink, have a glass of decaf iced tea, a glass of red wine, or water with lemon. For dessert, you can eat a raspberry sorbet.

Evening Fitness Exercise

After dinner, go on a twenty-minute walk and drink a glass of iced water with lemon. Also, do some muscle stretches and condition your body to feel at your best.

Evening Mental Exercise on the First Day

What number is next in the following sequence?

3 8 15 24 _____

Bedtime Snack

If you are used to eating a snack after dinner, eat a banana or a peanut butter and banana sandwich.

First Tuesday, Day Two

Breakfast

½ cup of hot oatmeal with brown sugar and blueberries

¼ cup of 2% milk or yogurt

one whole grapefruit

coffee, water, or orange juice

multivitamin supplement

Fitness Plan for the Day

If you usually park your car near your workplace, park or get dropped off far from where you need to go and then walk briskly to get to work. You can also add a five-minute walk. Instead of riding the elevator, take the stairs. Then, drink some water.

Morning Mental Exercise

Memorize the following list of words by looking at the paper and repeating them out loud at least 5 to 6 times.

Banner, Ditch, Heart, Spade, House

Mid-Morning Snack

Hard-boiled egg

1 cup of tomato juice

Green tea, coffee, or water

Mid-Morning Mental Exercise

Get out a pen and paper. Use your left hand if you are right-handed or vice-versa for the entirety of this exercise. First, draw the best circle you can. Now fill it in with your pen and try not to color outside of the circle. When you have completed it, sign your name on it.

Stress Relief in the Afternoon

Take a long walk, which will help you get out your negative feelings. If you are feeling stress, do some power walking. It will help release any tension in your body. Make sure to do some stretches, which will help you feel better.

Afternoon Snack

Have a banana with milk. You could also put some peanut butter on the fruit, which will help you feel more energetic.

Afternoon Mental Exercise

Write down a list of random words that you have encountered today. It could be any set of words. Put them in random order. Then study them and see what you come up with. Note if you can organize the whole list in order. Give yourself some time to do this and then come back to it later.

Dinner

Have a garden salad with balsamic vinaigrette and mix tuna in it or some other meat. Have some sweet potatoes and rolls for side dishes.

Evening Fitness Exercise

After dinner, go on a short jog or long walk of about 20 minutes. And make sure to drink some water when you get back.

Evening Mental Exercise

Do a crossword puzzle or play Scrabble with friends.

Bedtime Snack

Have a handful of almonds or walnuts.

First Wednesday, Day Three

Wake-Up Stretches and Brisk Walk

Begin with a brisk walk around the neighborhood, which will help you wake up and experience a fresh start to your day. Do some stretches and deep breathing exercises, which will get your body moving and help you get in shape. Drink a bottle of water.

Breakfast

1 Granny Smith apple

½ cup of cheese

250ml coffee or water

Morning Mental Workout

Go through and study a proverb with the goal of memorizing it. Choose one that will motivate you and help you remember what you need to do. Meditate on it and study it, then come back to it and try to recall each line of it by heart.

Mid-Morning Snack

Cut up a celery stalk into sticks. If you like, add peanut butter and raisins.

Lunch

Garden salad with grilled chicken, crackers, an orange, and tea.

Afternoon Stress Release

Sit in a chair and imagine that you are on a beautiful beach before sunset. Breathe in and out deeply and form in your mind the image of this picturesque place. Then, listen to the birds around you and the waves on the horizon. Then, focus your eyes and exhale deeply. Open your eyes and continue the rest of your day in concentration mode.

Afternoon Snack

1 cup of yogurt (you can use frozen yogurt)

½ cup of strawberries

water with lemon

Afternoon Mental Workout

Do you remember the words you studied yesterday afternoon? If you have forgotten, go back through them.

Dinner

Have some pan-seared salmon with lemon and also have an egg toast, which will be a delicious combination. On the side, have a large bowl of salad with broccoli, celery, and other greens. You could also add a raspberry vinaigrette.

Evening Stress Relief

Sit in a chair and take a deep breath and let it out, then tense up your different muscle groups. Release the tension. Allow yourself to relax through your cheeks and jaw and all the way down to your shoulders. Keep breathing and allow your whole body to feel the difference. Inhale and exhale. And do all of this with your eyes closed.

Evening Mental Exercise

Try to memorize an acrostic poem. Write out the letters of your name and create some adjectives to describe each one of them.

Then, look at it and try to memorize each letter of your name. Associate each of these letters with something tangible in your life. Then, come back to it later and write out all the letters of your name.

Bedtime Snack

Have a half of a peanut butter and jelly sandwich with a glass of milk.

First Thursday, Day Four

Wake-Up Stretches and Brisk Walk

Lie down on your back on a yoga mat and do some stretching with your back muscles. This will help you relax, fix your posture, and enable you to get on your feet faster. You can strengthen your core as well. Do some crunches and sit-ups on the floor.

Breakfast

Eat a whole-grain cereal with banana and low-fat milk. And drink a cup of hot coffee with no cream or sugar. Just black. You could also add an extra shot of espresso for a greater boost.

Fitness Plan for the Day

For today, we can emphasize doing a team sport later in the day. You could play basketball, tennis, soccer, or another team sport. Often, team sports will help you feel more confident and secure in yourself. Give it a try. This will make a difference in your life. If you don't get to do a team sport, try going outside and walking. It will clear your head. Try to get your step count up to 10,000. Or better yet, build it up to 12,000 steps.

Morning Mental Exercise

Take a phone book and start memorizing some phone numbers in the book. Take about five phone numbers from the book and try to recite them. Write them five times in a notebook. Then, try to recite them out loud and write them without looking at the book again.

Mid-Morning Snack

Have a bowl of granola with yogurt and blueberries on top. This is a simple but delicious mid-morning snack, which is sure to give you an energy boost when you're feeling physically or mentally tired.

Mid-Morning Mental Exercise

Do a crossword puzzle from the newspaper. Spend some time sharpening your logical reasoning skills. Alternately, do a word search. You can generate one of these online at Puzzlemaker.com. Enter the words you want to be in the search and generate the word search. Print it off and then do it. There is no answer sheet, but you can do it all yourself. It will be a good exercise in visual and spatial memory.

Lunch

Have a bowl of chili with kidney beans, ground beef, and tomato sauce. You can make this dish easily in a crockpot and allow it to cook all morning. You can add your favorite cheese or sour cream sauce to it, which will make it delicious.

Stress Relief in the Afternoon

Practice mindfulness in your room or at work at your desk. You can sit on a mat on the floor and meditate with quiet music and low lighting. Do this for about thirty minutes. Rest your head and if you get tired, take a short ten-minute nap.

Afternoon Snack

For an afternoon snack, you can have some walnuts or cashews. You might get a little thirsty, so I recommend a glass of water with it. Of course, you're staying well hydrated, so you don't need me to tell you to drink!

Afternoon Mental Exercise

Draw a map of your surroundings in your neighborhood. Go on an observation tour of your house and area where you live. Take in everything and observe what you see. You can take down notes or even sketch a mini diagram that you can remember. This is like taking pictures except in your mind. After you get back, do something else to create a buffer of time, and then sketch a drawing or map of what you saw on your tour of the neighborhood.

Dinner

Have some pasta carbonara with mozzarella cheese, bacon bits, and eggs. And you can cook some garlic bread in the oven. Also, have an all-greens salad with spinach, lettuce, and other things, drizzled with olive oil.

Evening Fitness Exercise

If you were not able to engage in a team sport today, go to the pool, take a walk, or go for a run. Implement one of these aerobic exercises for at least thirty minutes to one hour.

Build up your time and stamina, and you will see some good physical results. Allow those endorphins to fill your mind and heart.

Evening Mental Exercise

Work with a Rubik's Cube or a puzzle with different parts. Piece it together and form a shape of something.

Bedtime Snack

Peanut butter and banana sandwich or healthy popsicle

First Friday, Day Five

Morning Stretches

Go outside of your house and breathe in the morning air deeply. Do some stretches next to the wall of the building. Stretch your legs and arms.

Breakfast

Have a bacon, egg, and cheese biscuit with a green salad on the side with honey mustard sauce. And have a glass of iced coffee or tea. Then, have a few strawberries or a grapefruit.

Fitness Plan for the Day

Plan on working on your core muscles. That means doing some muscular exercises. You can go to the gym for this or you could do some exercises at home.

Do whatever you prefer. But make sure to work on your core during the day. You can find numerous resources on how to exercise at home.

Morning Mental Exercise

Rearrange your car with different locations for different things. Try to put your items somewhere where you normally don't. Then, try to remember where you put everything.

Mid-Morning Snack

Have an apple. You can put honey or peanut butter to add a little bit of sugar to it. It should give you a sweet boost to your morning.

Mid-Morning Mental Exercise

Do some math problems in your head. Write out some multiplication, division, or algebra problems.

If you need help with this, find a book (test prep or otherwise) and practice doing the calculations in your head without writing anything down.

This will help you logically reason through each step in your head and enhance your cognitive functions.

Lunch

Make a tuna fish sandwich on whole grain bread and use arugula to add some spicy flavor. Enjoy a handful of veggie chips and some dried fruit. Drink a cup of milk.

Stress Relief in the Afternoon

For your afternoon stress relief, you should do some meditation and reading and writing. After meditating or praying, read a little bit from your favorite book. Or, you can also write your thoughts down in a journal.

Afternoon Snack

Have a protein shake with your favorite fruit, such as grapefruit, berries, or others that you like. It should last you until the evening. You can have a light dinner.

Afternoon Mental Exercise

Play a game on the computer, phone, or video game. You can find a game that includes logical reasoning and is not too violent. Try to find a game that has problem-solving sets. It will help you with problem-solving skills in your daily life.

Dinner

You can have grilled cheese and tomato sandwiches with soup. Then, you can add your favorite vegetables on the side. Also, it has been shown that eating carrots is a beneficial vegetable to improve your eyesight. So, have some carrot sticks with your meal.

Evening Fitness Exercise

For your evening fitness exercise, you can do some simple stretches and running in place. Additionally, you could run or walk on the treadmill for 20 minutes. That should get your blood pumping and help you to feel better.

Evening Mental Exercise

Attempt the military method with a text you are trying to memorize. For example, you might be trying to learn a poem or short document. Go into your bathroom and turn out the lights and capture the image of the text in your brain. And then, try to both say and write out the text verbatim. It will be helpful to enhance your brain activity.

Bedtime Snack

An assortment of nuts can be your final food for the day.

First Saturday, Day Six

Wake-up Stretches and Brisk Walk

For Saturday, you can do more intense exercises because it is the weekend. Try to do some stretches on your bed or on a mat to strengthen your muscles and help with your flexibility.

Then, take a short brisk walk or jog outside to get your blood pumping and allow yourself more freedom in your exercise.

Breakfast

Have a bowl of oatmeal with brown sugar and raisins. Give yourself some daily coffee or tea to go with it. You could also pair it with a glass of cold orange juice.

Fitness Plan for the Day

Today, you should get involved with a team sport. For example, you could do a swimming team, basketball, baseball, or some other sport. Try to do a club activity with other people where you can get to know some new faces and names. This will enhance your brain activity and enable you to get to know other people who are also passionate about fitness. It will help you a lot. Join a sports team or other sports club to experience new things.

Morning Mental Exercise

For your morning mental exercise, you can play a musical instrument. Whether that is strumming a guitar, playing the piano, or jamming on the violin.

Find something that you like to do. Listen to a piece of music on your computer or phone. Try to play that same song by ear and from memory. This exercise will be helpful to your memory and get some neurons moving in your brain.

Mid-Morning Snack

For your mid-morning snack, you can have a granola bar that has multigrain nutrients and nuts. This will be good for your brain.

Mid-Morning Mental Exercise

You will do an exercise that will strengthen your memory. For example, you could practice memorizing words from a foreign language that you're learning.

Start associating words with concepts. Put word families together and memorize in chunks. Then, use some flashcards to review what you have learned.

Lunch

Have a light lunch, such as a grilled chicken salad or add beef to your plate. This will help you to have more energy. Add a banana or other fruit to your meal. Drink water or juice.

Stress Relief in the Afternoon

In the afternoon, you can practice some techniques you might learn in cognitive behavioral therapy classes. For example, try tensing up your muscles and then relaxing in a chair.

Focus on each muscle group in your body. Sit up straight in a chair and go through your body from head to toe. Be as tense as possible and then release the tension. Feel your body relax. Then you can go about your day as usual.

Afternoon Snack

You can have a banana or some strawberries for your afternoon snack. Just don't go too heavy on your snacking.

Afternoon Mental Exercise

To train your brain in the afternoon, try doing some word problems in your head. Find some online or in a test prep book.

If you're getting ready for the SAT or GRE, you can practice these problems on your own. Do not use a calculator or any other device. Rely on your brain and cognitive functions for this exercise.

Dinner

For dinner, have chicken parmesan that you can cook in the oven. Sprinkle parmesan cheese and tomato sauce on top of the chicken and bake it. You can also have some garlic bread with butter. Add a leafy salad with broccoli and other greens. For dessert, you can have a yellow custard that has dairy products.

Evening Fitness Exercise

In the evening, you can do some walking or running on the treadmill or outside in the neighborhood. Make it light and not too heavy.

Evening Mental Exercise

Watch *Jeopardy* or *Who Wants to Be a Millionaire*. Try out your trivia skill. Or you could try a game show online, which would help you to exercise your mental powers.

Bedtime Snack

Before heading off to bed, consider having an apple or banana.

First Sunday, Day Seven

Wake-up Stretches and Brisk Walk

Before you get your day started, begin with a short walk around the neighborhood.

If you have a dog, take him or her for a stroll. You can also walk and talk to a friend, spouse, or another special person in your life.

Breakfast

Have a light breakfast with granola or cereal and yogurt. Have strawberries or blueberries with it. This will be a good mixture of everything.

Fitness Plan for the Day

Because it is Sunday, you can rest from the physical activity today. So, just relax in your home. Take a long Sunday nap or hang around in your pajamas at home while watching TV.

Morning Mental Exercise

Again, because it is Sunday, you should make everything light. Do a simple exercise with logical reasoning and math. For example, find the next number in the following sequence.

5, 15, 45, 135 _____

(In this case, you would use multiplication to find the next number.)

Mid-Morning Snack

For your mid-morning snack, you could have some walnuts and a glass of water to satisfy your thirst.

Mid-Morning Mental Exercise

Now, you can try your hand at drawing or painting a picture. Look at some pictures of different things in a magazine or in a book. Then, try to copy the image by painting or drawing on a piece of paper. This enables you to have some creativity and fun.

Stress Relief in the Afternoon

Take a load off. Take a load off. Or do some chores around the house. You can vacuum or clean your room afterward, which will help your homestay in tip-top shape. You can also do some laundry in your home.

Afternoon Snack

Because you have not done too much activity, you don't need much food to sustain you. Instead, you could drink a glass of cold milk.

Afternoon Mental Exercise

For your afternoon mental exercise, you can try doing a crossword puzzle or work with a Rubik's Cube to get your mind working.

Dinner

Have some kind of fish that is either fried or grilled. You can have some vegetables on the side and have a bowl of multigrain rice. This will be a healthy meal for you in the evening.

Evening Fitness Exercise

None. Simply rest in your house.

Evening Mental Exercise

None. Simply rest your mind. Go to bed early.

Second Monday, Day Eight

Wake-up Stretches and Brisk Walk

Begin with a brisk walk around the neighborhood, which will help you wake up and experience a fresh start to your day. Do some stretches and deep breathing exercises, which will get your body moving and help you to do what you need to do to get in shape.

Breakfast

For breakfast, have a waffle with maple syrup and butter. And have a large glass of cold milk.

Fitness Plan for the Day

Today, work on aerobic fitness. That means doing swimming, running, or walking for at least 45 minutes. Build up your stamina and go farther than you did last week. This will help you work on endurance and enable you to keep going farther than you could before.

Morning Mental Exercise

For the morning mental exercise, start your day with a riddle or proverb. Try to solve the problem in your head and then write it down. Afterward, try to recite the information from memory without looking at your writing.

Mid-Morning Snack

Enjoy a slice of bread or toast with a nut butter.

Mid-Morning Mental Exercise

For your mid-morning mental exercise, try memorizing numbers and addresses of different buildings near your home. Look at a map and try to memorize each of them.

Stress Relief in the Afternoon

Do some meditation exercises in your room or in a quiet place wherever you may be. And then drift off into a brief five-minute catnap to get more alert.

Afternoon Snack

For a pre-dinner snack, try eating some banana chips. Don't overeat because it might spoil your dinner. Eat moderately.

Afternoon Mental Exercise

On a sheet of paper, write down two details you remember from your commute to work in the morning. As you return home or when you follow the same route tomorrow, look at this sheet of paper to see how you did.

Dinner

You can have vegetable lasagna. Put spinach in lasagna shells and create a beautiful mixture. Also, have some garlic rolls. And you can have a glass of wine with your meal.

Evening Fitness Exercise

After dinner, go on a twenty-minute walk. Also, do some muscle stretches and condition your body to feel at your best.

Evening Mental Exercise

Do a vocabulary-building activity. Read a difficult text and pick out the key words from it. Then, look up the definitions and put everything into a puzzle that you can solve on your own. This will help you to develop your problem-solving and lexical skills.

Second Tuesday, Day Nine

Wake-up Stretches and Brisk Walk

Do some stretches on the floor on a yoga mat and stretch your legs, arms, and other muscles. Then, go for a brisk walk outside before you go to work or hang out at home.

Breakfast

For Tuesday's breakfast, have some eggs and bacon and biscuits. A hearty breakfast with varied protein sources will give you lots of energy for the day.

Fitness Plan for the Day

Today's fitness plan should include some yoga or other light physical activity. You can plan it in your day. Try to go to the gym for a class or do some activity around your neighborhood.

Morning Mental Exercise

To strengthen your memory, read a book and listen to the audio version being read aloud. Allow yourself to follow the words on the page and increase your reading speed. Try to comprehend the whole thing as you're reading. Don't stop and look back at the words. Instead, keep reading and then after you finish the recording, try to write down every detail you can remember from the text and create a summary.

Mid-Morning Mental Exercise

For your mid-morning exercise, you can try to review the text that you had studied before. Think of some questions you would ask yourself of the text. Then, try to answer the questions on your own.

Stress Relief in the Afternoon

After lunch, try to do some mindfulness exercises at your desk or at home on your couch. Relax and take a load off.

Afternoon Snack

You could have a bowl of cereal or granola with fruit for a snack in the afternoon.

Afternoon Mental Exercise

You can now do a mental exercise with the words you learned on Saturday. Put them into a puzzle or word search and then solve the puzzle. Don't use any visual aid that could help you. Try to do it all on your own.

Dinner

Have a vegetable soup with cornbread or rolls. It could be a stew with multiple vegetables. Make it vegetarian. Then, have a fruit salad and macaroni salad for your side dishes.

Evening Fitness Exercise

In the evening, why not take a ball and play outside with friends or family? Play basketball or soccer in the park or neighborhood with people you know. Spend some time socializing and playing at the same time. It could help you.

Evening Mental Exercise

Rest your mind and get into bed early.

Second Wednesday, Day Ten

Wake-up Stretches and Brisk Walk

By now you should have a routine and be familiar with this start to your day.

Breakfast

Breakfast can be a simple piece of toast with jam and butter. You can also have a cup of yogurt with berries.

Fitness Plan for the Day

Today's fitness plan should include some moderate physical activity, including running, swimming, or walking for at least one hour. You can do this in your day. Integrate some time to do this during your routine.

Morning Mental Exercise

Before doing any work or the day's main activity, do a crossword puzzle or read an article in the newspaper. It will help activate your brain in the morning.

Lunch

Have a light lunch with a sandwich and yogurt.

Stress Relief in the Afternoon

If possible, spend some time relaxing at home or elsewhere. Have a nice cup of coffee in a cafe. Or, curl up with a book. Spend time doing some low-key activities. It will help you experience more stress relief.

Afternoon Mental Exercise

Your afternoon mental exercise should include some speed writing. Get the ideas flowing in your head. Reflect on everything you've experienced so far during the week.

Write everything down on a piece of paper and give yourself a few minutes to do that. Then, try to recite everything you wrote from memory.

Dinner

Use the same guidelines as you did last week. You can repeat a dish that you liked and make it. Or find a new recipe online that you can make with the ingredients in your kitchen.

Do so mindfully and without much stress. Enjoy the cooking process.

Evening Fitness Exercise

You should do an exercise that is light and fun. For example, you could go for a bike ride or you could use a stationary bicycle in the gym. Do some weight lifting or other activity to strengthen your muscles.

Evening Mental Exercise

Put together a puzzle or do something similar that allows you to use both your hands and your mind. Don't consume any bedtime snack. Simply drink a lot of water.

Second Thursday, Day Eleven

Wake-up Stretches and Brisk Walk

Breakfast

For breakfast, have some meat, eggs, and an English muffin or toast. Then, make a fruit parfait with yogurt. This will strengthen you, as you eat the most important meal of the day.

Fitness Plan for the Day

For today's fitness plan, we should integrate some light stretches, intensive aerobic activity, and some protein shakes to replenish our energy. This includes swimming, running, or walking.

Choose an activity you like and engage in it. But do so with an intense pace for only thirty minutes. Then, rest.

Morning Mental Exercise

For today, you can try memorizing some phone numbers of friends or family members. Recall these numbers effectively and commit them to memory. Try to create a jingle with the numbers using some of your favorite songs.

It will be fun and perhaps amusing if you share the results with your friends or family members.

Stress Relief in the Afternoon

For stress relief in the afternoon, try taking a short walk outside if it is not raining. Or, if indoors, you can just walk around and reflect on your day.

Think out loud and to yourself. It will help you clarify your thinking.

Afternoon Snack

For an afternoon snack, you can try having a banana and toast with honey or jam.

Afternoon Mental Exercise

For your afternoon mental exercise, try solving word problems you might find in a test-prep book or math textbook. Work these out using your brain and don't write anything down.

Dinner

Have a vegetarian pizza for dinner with spinach, peppers, green onion, and other veggies toppings. Make sure to use the highest quality cheese on top, as well.

Evening Fitness Exercise

Rest from your hard, intense exercise this evening. Read a book or watch a movie instead.

Evening Mental Exercise

Rest your mind from the activity that you have done this week.

Second Friday, Day Twelve

Wake-up Stretches and Brisk Walk

Breakfast

For breakfast, have a bowl of cereal or granola with berries on it and some milk. Also, drink a glass of cold orange juice.

Fitness Plan for the Day

Today's fitness plan includes playing a team sport with your neighborhood soccer, baseball, or basketball team. Even if you don't like to play sports, you should find a way to integrate sports into your routine. You can socialize with people around you and discover ways you can connect with others. On this last day of the week, find an activity you can do with another person. Alternatively, you could play table tennis, which involves two people.

Morning Mental Exercise

For this last day of the week, you should try to do some memorizing with texts. For example, memorize key lines from your favorite poem. Write it out five times. And then do some spaced repetition with it. You can extend this activity through the whole day and into the weekend.

Mid-Morning Snack

For your snack, try eating some nuts and a glass of water. Nuts have good nutrients that will help strengthen your brain and activate those neurons.

Mid-Morning Mental Exercise

Do some continued spaced repetition with the poem you want to memorize. Allow this to continue into the weekend.

Stress Relief in the Afternoon

For your afternoon stress relief, try taking a shower or cleaning yourself. Get dirty and sweat first doing an activity and then take a shower. Enjoy feeling your body relaxing and experiencing stress relief.

Afternoon Snack

Have an apple or some berries with yogurt. Simple but good.

Afternoon Mental Exercise

Continue to study the text that you have been working on memorizing for the weekend.

Dinner

Have some breakfast for dinner on this day. It will help you experience more strength and give you some comfort food. Have a breakfast casserole with sausage, eggs, and vegetables. It will be super-delicious.

Evening Mental Exercise

Evening mental exercises should include review of information that you have acquired today. You can also do a journal entry of all the activities you have done today. Write out everything you can remember from today.

Bedtime Snack

Before bed, have a milkshake with yogurt instead of milk and your favorite fruit, like mango, strawberry, or blueberry. Use real fruit in this shake. Then, have a cup of tea and go to bed early, so you can get an extra hour of sleep.

Second Saturday, Day Thirteen

For the second Saturday, you don't need to do a routine that is different from usual. Instead, you can follow the guidelines from the first week and do similar exercises the second week.

Continue to review all the things you learned this past week. Do some review mental exercises that will strengthen your memory. Recite by heart the poem that you started memorizing on Friday. And find a place where you can practice it and then perform before a live audience.

Make sure that you always do mindful eating and eat sensibly. Follow the guidelines on the right foods to consume in your routine. Add more vegetables, fruits, yogurt, and fish to your diet that you can have on the weekend. As for physical activity, continue to develop your skill in walking, running, or swimming. You can also practice the activity with friends and family in team sports.

Second Sunday, Day Fourteen

For the last day in your routine for memory enhancement, you should rest from all physical activity. You can review the poem and text that you were working on before. However, you should be careful not to overwork your brain. It is certain that you are likely tired from the "boot camp" experience that this has been for two weeks. Resting your mind will give your brain time to reassemble memories and experiences. It's essential that you sleep well and give yourself ample time to recover from various experiences you might have. So, on this day, give yourself a break, eat sensibly, sleep well, and conclude this week by relaxing on the sofa or reading a good book. You've worked so hard the past two weeks, and you should reward yourself for the reasonable efforts you have made in enhancing your memory.

Conclusion

Well, you've made it! Congratulations!

You have now gotten through the memory improvement action plan for two weeks! You did a great job! I know it must have been a bit of a challenge for you, but you faced the day with resilience, perseverance, and strength. It takes a long time to get through this period, but I know that these two weeks have likely flown by, and you have barely been able to catch your breath.

The activities in this section have included mindful eating, meditation, moderate to intense physical exercise, daily mental exercises, and review that enable you to achieve the results you want in enhancing your memory.

I know — and hopefully you know now, too — that by taking these steps, you can achieve a positive lifestyle change, which will help your memory to stay sharp. Whatever life stage you may be in, these activities will be beneficial brain exercises to help you stay fresh and achieve more.

Now that you're finished, go out and celebrate. Have dinner in the finest restaurant with friends and family. Go to the cinema and watch a movie, or hang out with friends. You deserve a reward for all this effort. Celebrate and party-hearty because the past two weeks have been a blast.

CHAPTER 16: 21 MEMORY IMPROVEMENT EXERCISES

As you continue to integrate these habits into your daily lifestyle, a variety of mental activities will help to keep your brain sharp. Our brains function almost like a computer. Whenever the brain is working the right way, then you can cognitively function well. However, if the opposite is true, then you will experience various problems. As we become older, our brainpower starts to go down. A perennial problem in today's world is dementia. Our brain wellness is just as essential as heart and lung health.

If you find that you are forgetting a lot of things, you might be greatly disturbed by it. But you don't have to feel that you are helpless because you can keep your brain healthy and you can improve its overall state.

A study in the journal *Neurology* talks about how older Americans who physically exercise their bodies every day are likely to be less affected by neurological disorders, which cause memory loss and limited mobility. On the other hand, people who engage in physical activity may be able to keep their brains strong and healthy and also reduce the risk of cognitive impairment. Let's now look at some brain exercises you can do every day to keep your memory sharp and healthy. If you're looking for more, David William (2018) offers more exercises in addition to these below.

Exercises to Sharpen Your Memory

1. Drive or Follow a New Route Home

It may seem trite and straightforward, but following a new route home will do wonders for your brain. If you get out of the routine movements of your life, your senses will be forced to discover the way home, which keeps your mind moving. Then you won't mindlessly go through the motions of going home without any reflection or consideration. You should avoid getting bored or putting your brain on autopilot. Mindless routines can cause us to get stuck and unable to move forward. Therefore, it is crucial to find ways to improve our overall mental state. Driving or walking home in a new way is going to give a boost to your mental sharpness.

2. Repeat Something Aloud

If you want to remember anything that you have just read, heard, or done, try repeating it aloud. For example, you might be talking to someone for the first time. You introduce yourself and then repeat his or her name. When you do that, you will be able to remember their name in no time. This also goes for reading. Often, it takes reading something aloud for us to commit it to memory. Sometimes, talking briefly out loud to yourself can be a helpful tool in enabling you to do all the things you want to do. Try doing that. It will save you a lot of hassle, and you might just be able to remember more things.

3. Listen to a Text While You Read

This method has been proven to help second language learners as they are reading a book in another language. You can try reading something to yourself silently in your native language while simultaneously listening to it read in the target language. When you use this method, you will engage your senses more and enable your mind to remember things a lot better. You can also do this with simple texts, as well. If you read along as someone else reads the version with you, then you will likely remember more from the text because you will have engaged your listening and reading skills.

4. Play Crossword Puzzles

One way that many people improve their memory is by playing word games and crossword puzzles. Games like Scrabble, where you can rearrange letters and make many words, will enable your brain to think more clearly, and you will be able to remember more. There is a reason why your grandparents would always do this. It is because when you play crossword puzzles, you allow yourself to assemble the words and concepts in your mind, which creates a vivid picture that will help you remember things better. Word games strengthen your vocabulary and enable you to do many things.

5. Play Chess

In addition to word games, don't forget to play strategy-based games like chess and checkers. When you play these games, you use your logical reasoning and strategy to master different situations. Additionally, you will feel more confident to handle all the things you need to do.

6. Learn to Play a Musical Instrument

Next, start to play a musical instrument. When you play an instrument like a violin or piano, you can engage the senses and remember something for a long time. Playing an instrument is also going to strengthen many of your other skills, including academics. It has been shown that playing a musical instrument can help a student get higher grades in school, which helps them greatly. It also makes a person well-rounded because they feel they can do all things well. It's a great confidence booster. Plus, just knowing different composers can be useful, as you can access the knowledge of music wherever you go. Music contributes to our mind's ability to concentrate more intently on things, as well. Study with a teacher. Join a band or orchestra. Do whatever it takes to make some music. You won't regret it for an instant.

Case Study

Wilson played the cello at school in Cleveland, Tennessee. He was very skilled and enjoyed playing with other people. In addition to his cello studies, he was gifted at math and science. Wilson wanted to be pre-med, so he put a lot of energy into becoming skilled in these subjects. Wilson got a perfect score on the SAT, and he credited a lot of his accomplishments to learning to play a musical instrument. He felt that by learning a stringed instrument that he expanded his range of knowledge and experience. He could concentrate more efficiently and learn different concepts faster. In addition, he played in an orchestra with other students. In this environment, he was well-supported by his teachers, and he got along well with his classmates. It greatly improved his overall experience in school and strengthened his memory.

7. Play a Sport

Some people like to play individual sports, while others like to do team sports. It all depends on the person, and you should do whatever suits you. Try a sport that builds your confidence and helps you to focus. If you're into individual sports, then try swimming or running. If you want to join a team, play basketball or some similar sport. It will help you improve your concentration. Athletic exercise helps improve both your physical health and your mental health. When you sweat at the gym, you will feel the effects both in your body and mind.

Case Study

Andrew liked to play basketball. His family was made up of athletes. He was a triplet and had two other brothers. All three of them were skilled at sports. It ran in the family. Andrew enjoyed learning new things and found that he could improve his study skills, as well.

He was gifted at math and got excellent grades in his Algebra 2 class. Andrew credited his skill in math to his involvement with sports. Through the physical and mental challenges of playing that sport, it helped him concentrate more in the classroom setting.

In addition to playing sports and math class, he was active in the scholastic academic bowl team, which competed regularly. He was able to answer questions on a variety of different topics. He also found that the principles of practicing, training, and discipline he learned on the practice field transferred to his efforts to develop as a member of the academic bowl team.

8. Learn a Foreign Language

Learning a foreign language enriches the mind deeply. The brainpower of a bilingual person is immensely powerful. When you can think about concepts in two or more languages, you are using your brain in a comprehensive way that maximizes its ability. Learning a foreign language is a fun thing, too. It can be easier than many think, and you can experience greater freedom than ever before because you can access other cultures through language. Besides, you can make more friends from different nationalities. When you learn a foreign language, you build your vocabulary and enable your mind to absorb the sights and sounds of a culture. This helps you to remember concepts and ideas in a more organized way. It challenges you to think outside the box and **experience new things. It is a win-win.**

Case Study

Anita learned how to speak French when she was in middle school. She remembers distinctly when she first heard French. She was in her class and her teacher required all students to speak French the whole time. It was hard for her at first, but eventually she was able to speak French fluently. It came naturally to her. She would memorize words and encounter new vocabulary each time.

The main way that she learned how to speak French well was through reading a lot in French. Anita read whatever she could in the language. She read the newspaper in French, books in the language, and went online to numerous French websites. Additionally, she watched French movies.

By the time she went to intensive language studies at Middlebury in Vermont and then eventually her time as an assistant English teacher in France, she had developed her fluency in French. She could speak it almost like a native.

Additionally, she worked on translations, which helped her to think in two languages at once. Through her bilingual skill, she was able to do well in college and graduated cum laude with a double major in the humanities and French. Her story was an amazing testimony of how hard work and dedication could pay off. The fact that she had committed so much time, energy, and money into learning French said a lot about her character as a hard worker and language student. Eventually, Anita became a high school French teacher in Tennessee. She went back to her childhood home and taught French to the students there. It was great for her to see how she had learned a lot over her short lifespan. Finally, Anita wanted to encourage the next generation to learn how to read, write, and speak in a foreign language. She advocated for second language learners and their newfound confidence in learning French.

9. Draw a Map of an Area from Memory

After visiting a new place, you can challenge your mind to remember by drawing a map of the place. Often, our brains capture images that can be remembered for ages to come. Once you return from visiting a place, you can remember all the sights and sounds of that place, which will help you continually be mindful of it. Also, you can draw pictures of your daily life, including your commute, neighborhood, and other parts of your routine, which will enhance your mind and develop your memory.

10. Learn How to Make a New Dish

Cooking is a skill that can be mastered by almost anyone, and it doesn't take too much effort. You can also take a cooking class to learn how to master a unique cuisine. When you cook, you stimulate different areas of the brain, which are associated with the senses, including smell, taste, and sight. Cooking can be a fun way to meet new people. Plus, you can enjoy the comfort of the food right at home. You won't have to go anywhere. Instead, you can have a great time cooking and make amazing dishes. You can also challenge yourself by trying out various new recipes without having to make the same thing over and over mindlessly. Instead, you allow your brain to try out new things. It's important to give your brain a boost. You won't regret it for an instant.

Case Study

Jason wanted to make a new dish, but he didn't know where to start. He felt that his cooking skills were rudimentary, and therefore he couldn't branch out and make something original. So, he went over to his friend Kevin's house. Kevin was a line chef at a restaurant in Boston, Massachusetts. He cooked many types of meals throughout his career. He was young and single, like Jason. Together, one evening, Kevin cooked pasta carbonara with Jason. Jason also made some garlic bread and a beautiful salad. It was a fantastic meal. Jason learned how to cook this meal, and he wanted to continue to cook because he thought that he could master this dish. Although it was the first time, he felt more confident about it after making it several times. Cooking something new would change his diet and also enable him to be more creative when preparing food in the kitchen.

11. Try Doing Your Chores with Your Eyes Closed

Instead of always doing your chores with your eyes open, try to do them with eyes closed. For example, you could wash the dishes, fold your laundry, or even take a shower with your eyes shut. When you do this, you will require your brain to use alternate ways to get the task done. However, you should not do anything with your eyes closed that could be dangerous to you or other people.

12. Eat Your Food with Chopsticks

We are all used to eating food with a fork and knife in the United States. It makes for an easy meal to eat. However, not every culture uses a fork and a knife. If you go to an Asian country, you may find yourself requesting a fork, but they often won't have them on hand. Therefore, learning to use chopsticks is a must. When you use chopsticks, you will activate your brain and enable it to do motor skills that you may have never used before. It is a helpful exercise for you. In addition to being challenging to your brain, it also helps you to be culturally sensitive and aware. Then, you can eat with chopsticks anywhere with any meal, especially in Asia. It's a great thing both mentally and culturally. Challenge yourself to use chopsticks today. When you order take-out from a Chinese restaurant, request chopsticks. You won't regret it.

Case Study

Emily was afraid to try new things. Then, she went to Asia, where she experienced a whole new way of life. Emily became an English teacher in Korea through the EPIK public school program. Emily was so used to using a fork and knife that she found it inconceivable for her to use chopsticks. She tried with all her might to learn while she was living in Boston and studying at Harvard. Nevertheless, she was not able to learn how to use chopsticks in the States, which made her a bit nervous about moving abroad to Asia. Once she arrived in Korea, she realized that she had to learn how to use chopsticks. It was not easy at first. And she had to ask to use a fork the first few months of her stay. Although people showed her how to use chopsticks, she failed to learn how. It was tough. She soon intuitively figured it out her way. It is not always an easy thing, but sometimes, one must learn by using intuition. Guided by this concept, a person can easily learn how to do almost anything. By watching and then adapting this technique, Emily learned how to use chopsticks. To this day, she is more adept at using chopsticks than a fork and knife, ironically enough. It is quite interesting, but it shows that Emily was able to move to a new country, adapt to her surroundings, and fit in among the locals. It's something that not everyone can do. This is one reason why moving to a foreign country is great for your brain.

13. Use Your Non-Dominant Hand Sometimes

We get used to using our dominant hands for any kind of function, whether that is brushing our teeth or eating with a fork. However, if you want to challenge yourself more, try using your non-dominant hand. It can be a bit hard at first, but then you will see how you can effectively train yourself to do this.

14. Meet New People

One way that you can enhance your memory is by meeting new people. When you meet a new person, you stimulate your brain and develop new ideas about the world. For some people, especially introverts, this task can be daunting. Some have trouble with names and faces and are therefore quite shy when around new people. However, if you can challenge yourself to meet and get to know more new people, you will feel more confident and able to engage with new ways of thinking. Widening your social circle will help you to have more friends, contacts, and people with whom you can find something in common. It helps bring you together with people who might be unlike you but could be very good to have as friends or acquaintances. Don't limit yourself only to your social circle. Try to break out sometimes and meet new people. You will find people to be much more helpful and interesting. And in some cases, you might meet a friend for life.

Case Study

Frank was a shy and introverted man. He did not naturally approach other people. Instead, he often would allow people to come up to him. It was difficult for him to get to know others, because he always found himself hiding behind closed doors. He went to a church and got to know people there, but he was always afraid of getting to know others. Frank was part of an international fellowship at his church. He wanted to get active in his involvement there. So, he decided to join the organization. The leaders approached him and asked him if he wanted to become a small group leader, which entailed leading studies with a small group on books, as well as welcoming new members. Frank was quite shy, and this task seemed daunting to him. He didn't want to get to know other people because of his introversion. But then, he took on the task gladly and succeeded in welcoming people into the group. It was difficult at first, but he had a lot of support from the other members of the organization. Soon, he was playing violin for the music team, and he felt that he had overcome a lot of personal obstacles. Fortunately, he was able to face his fears and overcome personal anxiety to accomplish many remarkable things in his life.

15. Practice Mindful Eating

Another thing you can do is practice mindful eating. This means savoring each and every meal you have. Identify the different ingredients in your food, including spices, salt, and other tastes. When you mentally go through the process of tasting and experiencing the food, then you will enjoy your meal more. Plus, you will be a more "live to eat" kind of person, rather than "eat to live." It helps to be someone who greatly appreciates food. That is what makes life worth living. When you go to a restaurant alone or with other people, take time to taste the food genuinely. Allow your taste buds to absorb the flavors and be mindful of every bite you take. You may feel like you're always in a hurry, but you should slow down sometimes and enjoy the moment. It will feel a little bit awkward at first because we live in such a fast-paced culture. But you can do it!

16. Try to Do Math Problems in Your Head

In today's world, we're often rushing to the calculator and using a pen or pencil to find out the answers to math problems. But if you want to help yourself remember better, try doing them in your head. Better yet, do it while walking or some other physical activity. When you can multitask and give yourself more time to do it, you will find that it will strengthen you and give you more mental energy.

Case Study

Jasper was a master mathematician. He earned a master's degree in pure mathematics from an elite university in the US. Because he was so gifted, Jasper could remember many different things. He didn't easily forget names of people or numbers that he had encountered. Because he was actively calculating figures in his head, he could always estimate how much money he was spending, which helped him to make budgets and plans. As a result, he did very well and wouldn't have any financial difficulties. Jasper loved to solve even basic mathematical problems daily. It was stimulating to his mind and helped him to remember details from his life. He experienced an amazing transformation and became aware of how he could effectively master all areas of life. His confidence grew, and he became a much more competent individual.

17. Practice Meditation

Sometimes we need to be quiet and concentrate our minds on softness. With our world that cannot stop talking, we need to have the space to be quiet and meditate. When you sit in silence and allow yourself to be mindful of your surroundings, then you will feel much better about things in your life.

Benefits of meditation include stress relief, improved concentration, memory enhancement, and the reversal of cognitive decline. Meditation has a place in your life. You don't necessarily have to be sitting down, Indian-style on a yoga mat. It can be writing things down, taking a walk, or finding other ways to let out stress. Practicing meditation can greatly enhance your life. You will be able to handle all different kinds of situations, and you will be able to conquer the negative emotions in your life.

A crucial complement to meditation is having a positive mindset. It's always important to be positive in whatever situation you face. Sometimes we act in negative ways, and we might also be caught up by many negative emotions, but we have to stop ourselves from flying off the handle. When you meditate or spend time praying or doing other related activities, you will feel much better and more relaxed. Then, you will be able to tackle any challenge you may face in your life.

Case Study

Daniel was a short-tempered child. He would often get into trouble at school. His emotions could easily overpower him at any given time. This caused him to throw temper tantrums in public and at school. The teachers were patient with him and helped him deal with his emotions. Then, Daniel's mother took him to the psychiatrist to get his condition checked out. Daniel was pretty normal overall; however, he needed to see a counselor who could help him navigate his complex emotions. His therapist helped him to understand what he was feeling. He also helped him to learn CBT (cognitive behavioral therapy), which helped him when he was troubled. Through practicing mindfulness, Daniel felt better and was less stressed. He learned the skill of meditation. With the help of the therapist, he practiced guided meditation every day for six weeks. Then, he could calm himself and feel more relaxed. He was ready to face the day. In addition, his memory experienced many benefits. Although he was a forgetful child due to his stressful emotions, he became able to remember things much more quickly and easily.

18. Memorize Phone Numbers and Other Figures

You can strengthen your memory by memorizing the phone numbers and names of people in your life. It will be an important difference you can experience. Often, we can divide ten-digit numbers into smaller sections, enabling you to remember better. If you break them up into groups of three or four, then you will know the number well. For example, try memorizing the number 222 435 7890. It is easier to remember when you group it that way than it is for you to remember 2224357890. When our brain sees large figures, we might easily be overwhelmed. However, when we break things up into chunks, then our brains can process the information faster and more efficiently.

19. Do Arts and Crafts

Crafts, such as drawing, painting, or knitting are becoming more popular because they can boost our brainpower. Whenever you take up one of these hobbies, you will strengthen your fine motor skills and enable your brain to think more effectively. Doing a craft allows us to think creatively. When you are creative, then you allow your mind to think freely and out of the box. You are no longer confined to simple things. Instead, you can strengthen your mind's ability to reason and do other activities. Be creative. Draw a picture or paint on a canvas. You will find yourself expanding your range of possibilities. Use your imagination. You can do it!

20. Tell Stories and Recite Poetry

Telling a story is one of the most important ways you can remember information. It helps you to remember all different kinds of things in your life clearly. You can also recite a poem by heart. When you do this, you will be memorizing not just the words but how to pronounce them. It will greatly improve your cognitive functions. It can also help improve your life if you or a loved one is struggling with Alzheimer's disease or dementia. It can mitigate the effects of neurological disorders, which can be challenging to live with. Therefore, find ways of integrating the recitation of stories and poetry in your routine, and you will find yourself able to do more things.

Case Study

Karin loved to study poetry. She was a poetry nerd. In school, she memorized many different poems, which helped her to ace different tests. As she regularly committed poems to memory, she found that she could remember a lot of details and events in her life. She continually recited Wordsworth, Coleridge, and Mallarme. She could never forget those lines. One day, she wanted to recite "The Highwayman," so she spent a few weeks memorizing the whole poem. It is a very long poem, so it was quite impressive that she could remember every line. For the next poetry slam at her school, she recited the whole thing out loud. And what do you know, everyone shouted "bravo!" with thunderous applause. It was amazing

21. Create an Acronym and Use Mnemonic Devices

Next, try to come up with your own mnemonic devices, which will make remembering things much easier for you. When you create original acronyms and mnemonic phrases, you train your brain to recognize the first letter of words and associate them with phrases or adjectives. When you make this connection, it will enhance your memory's power and let you do amazing things.

Case Study

Gerald liked to use acronyms to remember the names of his students in a class. During one of his class sessions, he had students describe their personalities and write out an acrostic poem for their name. After the lesson, Gerald took the cards, took a picture of the entire classroom, and then recalled the details of the class. He looked at the class and the seating chart and was able to identify each of the students. While getting to know each of his students personally, he found that he could form relationships with them and make lasting memories. He held the keys to relational success in the classroom. The students appreciated him and found that he was a helpful, kind, respectful, and social teacher. This helped them to learn their subject more effectively.

Other Things You Can Try to Do to Help You Remember

Visualize to Help Your Remember

Say you need to remember to buy a loaf of bread from the bakery. You can picture this item on your list and imagine that the loaf of bread is on your head, an egg is in your hand, a sushi roll is on your shoulder, etc. Find ways of making it creative. Use your body to remember things. And then, take a mental picture of it, so it won't be that difficult to recall what you need to buy. You will easily be able to remember.

Change Up Your Surroundings

If you want to remember more clearly and effectively, try changing up things like your routine and surroundings. Play some music in the background, if you don't typically do that. Or, do things like walk and think at the same time. When you think, your surrounding is crucial. When you put things in a context, you will be more likely to remember based on those things around you. Change up your room and put items in different places. You will test your brain's ability to remember where things are. It can help enhance your memory.

Space Out Learning Sessions

Cramming is not a good way to learn new information. It's not going to help you remember too much. Nonetheless, many people rely on this method to get them through school and remember imperative terms for an exam. If you want to remember things like foreign language vocabulary, dates, definitions of scientific words, or statistical data, then slowly space things out. When you do this, you will learn and remember more things. Spaced repetition is an essential way to help you recall information for a test. Don't think you can wait until the last minute to study for an exam and remember everything. You might be able to regurgitate the information by the time the test comes, but you won't be able to remember anything after the test is over. To learn more, study something a little bit at a time repeatedly. Then, it is likely you will remember the information for a long time, or if memory serves you well, for the rest of your life.

Get Some Shut Eye

One final thing you need to do to help your memory is to get sufficient sleep. You won't be able to remember well if you don't get enough sleep at night. Your brain needs to have at least six to eight hours of sleep per night to function properly. If this doesn't happen, your brain might have some misfirings and other things that can affect your ability to do normal tasks. Your brain needs some time to process and consolidate the information in your permanent memory bank. When you sleep more, you will find that you can remember a lot better. So, do it; get some shut eye. It's not selfish or unnecessary. It's essential for a better life.

CONCLUSION

Through a combination of factors, we can enhance our memories. Like our bodies, they need training and habits that promote greater well-being. We must learn to take care of our memories like we would our physical body. Better memory can be achieved. You can boost your memory and learn faster and be more productive and gain more knowledge.

Perhaps you want to have better focus and a higher level of concentration to avoid wasting time and energy at work. Maybe you also want to have a photographic memory to remember all kinds of facts and details about people and material objects. Also, you may have wanted to train your brain to avoid memory loss.

In this book, I have shown you the steps to take to improve your memory and have a photographic memory. I have given you the rundown of how to do it step-by-step, with an action plan that guides you through the process. I have demonstrated how it is possible to improve your memory and boost cognitive functions through the foods you eat, the amount of sleep in your routine, the daily habits you cultivate, as well as other factors. We have shown you tricks of the trade that enable you to remember more, think and learn faster, and use special memory improvement exercises. If you follow this advice, you will likely be able to see results in your overall mental function.

This guide has been practical and filled with useful tips, methods, and exercises to help you learn more. Instead of focusing on theory, I have shown how you can use research-proven methods to achieve the results you want. In addition, I revealed a two-week action plan that will help you immediately start improving your memory. Through this foundation, you will get real-life and instant results.

Through following this plan and going step-by-step, we know you will see a dramatic improvement in your memory. Your brain needs training. Work out frequently. Train yourself to learn more about the world every day. Be curious. Be daring and brave. Explore the crevices of this vast and fascinating universe. As a lifelong learner, you will have a sharper memory that will take on anything. For the rest of your days, you can enjoy more significant cognitive function than ever before. You can always have the brain of a 25-year-old and be healthier.

Thank you for joining me on this journey to memory development and improvement. I hope that you will take the actionable steps to improve your memory and live a fruitful and meaningful life filled with joy and peace.

REFERENCES

Ano, Y., & Nakayama, H. (2018). Preventive Effects of Dairy Products on Dementia and the Underlying Mechanisms. *International journal of molecular sciences*, *19*(7), 1927. doi:10.3390/ijms19071927

Boureston, K (n.d.) How to Develop a Photographic Memory: The Ultimate Guide. [blog] Mantelligence. Retreived from https://www.mantelligence.com/how-to-develop-a-photographic-memory/

Bullard, A. (n.d.) Ten Ways to Increase Your Reading Speed. Lifehack. Retreived from https://www.lifehack.org/articles/productivity/10-ways-increase-your-reading-speed.html

Charlie Brown Christmas: Lucy Van Pelt (n.d.) IMDB. Retrieved from https://www.imdb.com/title/tt0059026/characters/nm0833559

Chernyak, P. How to Avoid Forgetting. Wikihow. Retrieved from https://www.wikihow.com/Avoid-Forgetting

Eidetic memory (n.d.). In *Wikipedia, The Free Encyclopedia*. Retrieved from, from https://en.wikipedia.org/w/index.php?title=Eidetic_memory&oldid=908833167

Foer, J. (2012). TED Talk: Feats of Memory Anyone Can Do. [Video] Retrieved from https://www.youtube.com/watch?time_continue=905&v=U6PoUg7jXsA

Heerema, E. (2019). Foods that Reduce the Risk of Dementia. Verywellhealth. https://www.verywellhealth.com/foods-that-reduce-dementia-risk-98464

How to Count Cards, n.d. The Memory Page. Retrieved from http://www.thememorypage.net/how-to-count-cards/

How to Memorize a Deck of Cards (2019). Wikihow. Retrieved from https://www.wikihow.com/Memorize-a-Deck-of-Cards

Lickerman, A. (2009) Eight Ways to Remember Anything. Psychology Today. Retrieved from https://www.psychologytoday.com/us/blog/happiness-in-world/200911/eight-ways-remember-anything

McKay, B., and K. (2019). Your Concentration Training Program: 11 Exercises that Will Strengthen Your Attention.

The Art of Manliness. Retrieved from https://www.artofmanliness.com/articles/your-concentration-training-program-11-exercises-that-will-strengthen-your-attention/

Memorizing Dates and Numbers, Mnemonic Tricks (n.d.). Archimedes' Laboratory. Retrieved from http://www.archimedes-lab.org/memorizing_numbers.html

Memory. (n.d.). Queensland Brain Institute: The University of Queensland, Australia. Retrieved from https://qbi.uq.edu.au/brain-basics/memory

Mnemonic. Merriam Webster Dictionary Online. Retrieved from https://www.merriam-webster.com/dictionary/mnemonic

Noyes, A (1947). The Highwayman. The Poetry Foundation. Retrieved from https://www.poetryfoundation.org/poems/43187/the-highwayman

Pegging Memory System (n.d.). Newline Ideas. Retrieved from http://www.newlineideas.com/personal-pegging-memory-system.html

Person-Action-Object-System, n.d. Memory Techniques Wiki. Retrieved from https://artofmemory.com/wiki/Person-Action-Object_(PAO)_System

Peterson, D. (2016). How I Memorized An Entire Chapter from Moby Dick. Vox. Retrieved from https://www.vox.com/videos/2016/12/28/14063674/memory-palaces

Poe, E.A. (1845). The Raven. The Poetry Foundation. Retrieved from https://www.poetryfoundation.org/poems/48860/the-raven

Power Up: One Day Brain Boosting Meal Plan (2017). BestMedicine. Retrieved from https://bestmedicinenews.org/recipes/power-up-one-day-brain-boosting-meal-plan/

Psych Central Staff (2018). Memory and Mnemonic Devices. Psych Central. Retrieved from https://psychcentral.com/lib/memory-and-mnemonic-devices/

Rosenbloom, C. (2018). Ten Foods That Can Help Fight Dementia. Chatelaine. Retrieved from https://www.chatelaine.com/health/foods-that-fight-dementia/

Small, G. (2005). **T**he Memory Prescription: Dr. Gary Small's 14-Day Plan to Keep Your Brain and Body Young [eBook] Hachette.

William, D. (2018). 25 Brain Exercises for Memory That Actually Help You Remember More. Lifehack. Retrieved from https://www.lifehack.org/804141/brain-exercises-for-memory

Made in United States
North Haven, CT
27 June 2024